Virgo

A Monthly Channeled Guide for the Year Ahead

(The Ultimate Guide to an Amazing Zodiac Sign in Astrology)

Twila Barrett

Published By **Phil Dawson**

Twila Barrett

All Rights Reserved

Virgo: A Monthly Channeled Guide for the Year Ahead (The Ultimate Guide to an Amazing Zodiac Sign in Astrology)

ISBN 978-1-77485-574-4

No part of this guidebook shall be reproduced in any form without permission in writing from the publisher except in the case of brief quotations embodied in critical articles or reviews.

Legal & Disclaimer

The information contained in this ebook is not designed to replace or take the place of any form of medicine or professional medical advice. The information in this ebook has been provided for educational & entertainment purposes only.

The information contained in this book has been compiled from sources deemed reliable, and it is accurate to the best of the Author's knowledge; however, the Author cannot guarantee its accuracy and validity and cannot be held liable for any errors or omissions. Changes are periodically made to this book. You must consult your doctor or get professional medical advice before using any of the suggested remedies, techniques, or information in this book.

Upon using the information contained in this book, you agree to hold harmless the Author from and against any damages, costs, and expenses, including any legal fees potentially resulting from the application of any of the information provided by this guide. This disclaimer applies to any damages or injury caused by the use and application, whether directly or indirectly, of any advice or information presented, whether for breach of contract, tort, negligence, personal injury, criminal intent, or under any other cause of action.

You agree to accept all risks of using the information presented inside this book. You need to consult a professional medical practitioner in order to ensure you are both able and healthy enough to participate in this program.

Table of contents

Chapter 1: Understanding Astrology 1

Chapter 2: Do I Really Belong To A Virgo? 4

Chapter 3: The Symbology Virgo 7

Chapter 4: Refine Your Sign 13

Chapter 5: The Three Decans 18

Chapter 6: The Cusps 27

Chapter 7: General Advice 31

Chapter 8: Scorpio, Your Astral Love Compatibility 105

Chapter 9: What Are The Stones From The Virgo Sign? 150

Chapter 10: What's The Color Virgo's Most Adored? 156

Chapter 1: Understanding Astrology

Astrology is derived out of the two Greek terms: "astro" and "logos." They refer to "stars" as well as "language in turn. Therefore, we can understand this word to refer to "the languages of stars."

To comprehend this language, it is necessary to gaze up, especially in the evening so that you can actually see the stars. We all know about The Big Dipper and Orion, but did you know that all the twelve zodiac signs can also be considered constellations? Different cultures have created their own constellations. However, we in the West we are able to recognize the 88 constellations.

Our planet is orbited by the sun, however from our perspective it's the sun that is the one doing the circular orbit. The path the sun travels through the skies is referred to as the ecliptic plane. Actually, all planets that orbit our solar system travel along this plane and that is the reason astrology charts can be made.

Out of the 88 stars that exist, thirteen are on the ecliptic's plane However, only twelve of them are utilized. Why? From our perspective the ecliptic's plane is a circle similar to a belt or vast ring of sky. A circle is composed of 360o, which makes it simpler to divide 360 by 12 , instead of 13. This way we divide our sky into equal portions with 30o of each.

When the sun travels over the skies, each one of the twelve constellations serves as a backdrop for it. Because the constellations have different sizes and shapes and shapes, the sun cannot spend the exact amount of time traveling through each one. It's in Virgo for 45 days. Virgo as an example however, it only spends 7 days when it's in Scorpio.

To address this issue, Ophiuchus, the thirteenth constellation, was eliminated. This enabled the ancient Astrologers to assign a uniform time for all twelve signs in the zodiac.

In case you're in doubt, Ophiuchus symbolizes the snake-holding man and is situated in opposition to Orion. If we include it in the astrological system we would put Ophiuchus in between Sagittarius or Scorpio. If you're located in the northern region of the globe the best time to view it during summer.

When you were born the sun was making its way across that constellation called Virgo. The sun did this by first going out of Libra and then, when it is out of your sign, it will enter Leo. It's based on how far away it is from other signs you have when the time you're born other traits may "bleed" into yours that can also have an impact on your.

Chapter 2: Do I really belong to a Virgo?

The astrology we in is used in the West uses today comes in the form of the Babylonians (now an integral part of modern-day Iraq) that lived about three thousand years ago. While later civilizations (like that of Greeks) have added their own ideas throughout the millennium, the method we continue to use today was derived from the first Babylonian model.

In 2010, Astronomers who were part of The Minnesota Planetarium Society claimed that we've been doing the wrong way. The axis of our planet has changed through the millennium, and will continue to change because planets do, it seems this is a process known as tilt axial.

What does this mean is it means that North Pole isn't always where it is or will stay exactly where it is. Since the Babylonians invented the concept of astrology, this zodiac's position has moved upwards by approximately 1 month. This means that we've all been plotting the path of the sun through the twelve zodiac signs in a way that's not correct (though recently some astrologers are noting Ophiuchus).

The geeky stuff is left aside This means that the sign you believe that you were born with was not really the one you ought to have been born under. Did you miss that? head?

According to Minnesota Astronomers, the following is an accurate and current method to identify your astrological sign

CapricornJan 20 - February 16AquariusFeb 16 - - March 11

Pisces March 11 Aries - April 18Aries April 18 to May 13

TaurusMay 13 through June 21GeminiJune 21 to July 20

June 20 Cancer - August 10Leo Aug 10 - September 16

Virgo Sept 16 - Oct 30LibraOct 30 - Nov 23

ScorpioNov 23 - 29OphiuchusNov 29 - Dec 17

SagittariusDec 17 - Jan 20

There's one issue with this. The astrology which is practiced in the West has been using in the last century has changed.

Western Astrology is dependent on the zodiac of tropical origin, which is set with the changing seasons. It is also aligned with the equinoctial point meaning it's not changing. The sidereal zodiac utilized for the East is fixed to the constellations -- and this will be the only one which must actually change.

What it means to the reader is that, if their horoscope happens to be built around the Western zodiac of the tropical (and If you're American or European one, it most likely is) Do not be worried. It's still Virgo!

If you're still inclined to be a Virgo and you're still thinking of yourself as a Virgo, let's move.

Chapter 3: The Symbology Virgo

The word "virgo" can be described as the Latin word that means women who are virgin (regardless the gender) however, it's connected to the term "virga," which means "young shoot," for a plant. However, in common usage it could also mean "self-contained," which is almost the most common characteristic of people born in this sign.

If you conduct an Google image search on that constellation, you'll be able to understand why the sign typically shows the image of a woman lying down, as if sitting on a sofa (like the upper-class Romans were at mealtimes). Similar to the upper class of Roman ladies, Virgos tend to be meticulous in their appearance and behavior and are generally quiet and shy.

This is why they can be perceived as being difficult to understand at the very least, or arrogant at worst. It's not always the case however they can't resist emitting the "keep your distance or otherwise" images.

This is why some Virgo women may wonder why, despite their attractiveness some people are approached however they are not. Some women are aware of sending out signals that read "back off, I'm talking about this" signal, yet are unable to keep from doing it since they don't really know what to do.

The traditional representation of Virgo is an homage to Astraea (Star Maiden) who was believed to be Justice, the Goddess of Law. Dike (pronounced"dee-kee" not "daik -- however, it's true that she's the one we get the phrase to mean "lesbian" in the first place). The story goes that in Greek mythology Astraea is the final god to leave the earth after she left after the Silver Age ended and ushered into the sinful and violent Iron Age (the current one that we're living in).

Because of this, Virgos are also associated with love and the earth. When things get tough, Virgo women are usually the ones who are last to start moving. Although this is a good idea and practice, it's not always a good thingparticularly in the case of toxic relationships, dead-end jobs, or hopeless circumstances. In the end, Virgo ladies are known for their stubbornness.

The traditional representation of Virgo typically depicts an image of a woman with either a sheaf or a sack of wheat. It represents experience, wisdom and wealth. It also suggests that she is an independent woman. This isn't the type of girl who is dependent on anyone else for food.

This wheat bundle also reveals another characteristic to what makes a Virgo woman. Because Virgo women possess a strong individualist streak and aren't able to reveal themselves to other people in a way that they can They are terrified from being dependent upon other people. This leads to three key traits.

The second is the fact that Virgo women are extremely driven and materialistic. The issue isn't money or the bling they're looking for in and of itself. It's the sense of safety in independence, power, and security that money can bring.

The second reason is that Virgos possess a large amount of respect for rank and order. Tradition, law and customs give them the security they seek. While they can be overwhelming for certain people are the very environment that Virgos flourish in. It's not a good idea to keep the people out and making money if there's no institutions to enforce one's wishes and safeguard property since it's all about property.

In addition, Virgos are very analytical and are essential to an agriculturally productive production. They are not a fan of chaos, which is why they conduct themselves in a systematic manner. This is evident in the care they show in their appearance and behaviour as well as their sense of aesthetics, as well as in their method of working.

Methodical is a different key word that can be used to comprehend Virgos. Each of the twelve signs is tied to an element and, as was mentioned earlier Virgo is one of the elements of earth.

Maybe Virgo woman's strength could be her weak point. The astrological symbol of this sign is the letter "M" that has a kind of loop in the middle. The two arches in the symbol symbolize wings, which are often featured in representations of Virgo.

This implies that she's not just a regular woman and is in a high position above the rest of us. Virgo woman's natural inclination to be reserved puts her on a pedestal however, as the saying is: "it gets very lonely when you're at the highest level."

Because it's lonely in the top the Virgo woman can feel disconnected and in a state of disconnection. The result is some becoming disengaged as well as cold, skeptical and inflexible. and irritable. It's not uncommon for Virgo women to experience relationships problems or even not are experiencing them at all.

If you're wondering about the loop at the top of the loop beginning, that's when it becomes extremely complex and sexist. Many believe that it is a symbol of the woman's crossed legs. It signifies "DO NOT ENTRY," which is why Virgo is a reference to virginity. Get it? Others believe it refers to the self-contained nature of this symbol is a symbol of.

The loop however expands into two tails similar to the spread legs. Also the natural reserve of Virgo is somewhat of a sham. Behind that protective wall lies an incredibly passionate woman with the capacity to give affection that she's very selective about whom she'll give the love to.

The women of the Virgo are typically in a state of conflict over all things. They are frank, yet inwardly enthusiastic Analytical and logical however, they are emotionally hungry. They are also ambitious yet respects hierarchy. There's no reason to be surprised that you're here, is it? You're a pity...

Chapter 4: Refine Your Sign

As there were numerous factors in the astrology of your birth that influenced your personality when that you were born. It might be a surprise if you were in a position to connect to every aspect mentioned in the preceding chapter. There are Virgos for instance and they are messy, loud-mouthedand out-of-control slobs. What is the reason for this?

Remember the introduction that explained the significance of your internal mental landscape? Also, remember how the proximity of a sign to other signs can affect the way that this internal map is created? Remember, too, the explanation for why the sun does not have an equal length of time within every zodiac sign?

Wonderful! If you're not about to claim that the hospital has gotten your birth certificate in error Let's try a bit refinement to maximize the value of your birth certificate.

The best method for doing this is to hire an astrologer to design your own personalized chart of the exact date, time and location of birth. In addition, there are several other factors to think about.

While Virgo generally covers the time period of the period from August 23 to September 22 it's actually a quite a bit more complicated than the other. This is the reason they release the new books each year. They must refresh the information according to the meteorological data that is in the picture for that particular year.

The sun enters Virgo in the early hours of August 21 however, the changes do not become apparent until many more days. Typically, Virgo comes into its full strength around the time of August 29 and stays in full force until September 20. Then, the influence starts to diminish for another seven days before it is when the influence of its next sign (which happens to be Libra) starts to be felt.

While we are able to divide the ecliptic's ecliptic plane into twelve distinct divisions that are each made up from 30o angles, the results of each sign aren't always as clear-cut. The official line between the signs is known as cusp (Latin for "spear" or "point") however, these were created for convenience and to guarantee uniformity. This is the reason why the sun may traverse a cusp or, alternatively, straddle two signs at once.

This is why every sign is divided into three decans, which is the Latin word meaning "ten." Also, 1o to 10o is more similar to the sign that preceded it in Leo and is known as the first decan. 11o-20o represents the next decan, and it is the time when the typical characteristics of Virgo are at their best as well as 21o to 30o can be considered the third. This is the point at which the traits of Libra begin to be absorbed into.

Astrologers are of the opinion (even those who follow an alternative Zodiac) they are eight kinds of Virgos:

1.) There's the workaholic , messy type who enjoys tools and can be a tech-savvy kind of guy that likes to spend time with while they play in their garage or at their laptops,

2.) There's the type of person that lives inside her heads, and can't be motivated to eat regularly, dress nicely or comb her hair or even clean her home and car.

3.) There's the caring Mother Theresa type who'll go out into conflict zones to aid both sides, or even be willing to take on more kids that Angelina Jolie,

4.) There's the artist who always has glue or paint on her hair or fingers and hair, so don't begin to work on her home or work area,

5.) There's the kind of person who must do everything at the correct time and in the right sequence, or else she's a mess,

6.) There's the literary and art critic. This Virgo is the type that has many admirers but has few real acquaintances because she can't be a writer or an art literary critic.

7.) There's the facts-and-figures archivist librarian kind who keeps track of everything, from the fact that you didn't present her with a present on her birthday 11 years ago, even though she bought you one every year. And finally,

8) There's also the Virgo who is most Leo than Libra to truly be part of the Virgo club.

There's too little time to talk about all the elements that influence a person's mental state and habits However, we can examine some of the most important ones.

Chapter 5: The Three Decans

Each decan is roughly 10 days. However, during this time it's not only the sun's rays that travel through Virgo. Other planets also speed through, further giving their unique influence on this sign. To make the situation complicated moon has to make its voice heard however it's becoming too complicated for our needs.

The planet that dominates Virgo the most is Mercury. Mercury was the god of messengers in the Roman pantheon, and whose Greek name was Hermes. Whatever you want to identify his name, the god was accountable in delivering the prayers of the gods and delivering their response (if there was one) and the person who assisted those who died go to the afterlife and was known for his the ability to think, be clever and intelligence.

While Mercury has the greatest influence over Virgo but its influence on the people born under this sign isn't total. As the sun travels through the Virgo area, Mercury's influence can be altered, shared or even diminished by other planets that are passing through for a short time.

First Decan The first Decan will run from August 23 until September 1

Mercury's influence is the strongest in this moment, and people born in this time are naturally communicators- masters of spoken and written word. Women born during this time make excellent speakers, teachers, writers diplomats, lecturers, lawyers and sales representatives.

They also make fantastic scam artists, liars and manipulators. While they are generally smart it is common for first decans to appear more capable, intelligent or even more profound than they actually are. This is due to Mercury who is the god of thieves, liars and poets, though not necessarily in the same order.

Because Virgo has the rank of sixth and consequently being the one with the highest degree of balance of all twelve there is a tendency to play the role of peacekeeper. While this is a good thing however, it also requires some control. If not controlled, the first can women become too controlling and obsessive about the cleanliness of their homes, or may get into conflict with.

Have you ever seen pictures or statues of a naked man sporting the wings of his feet holding an oblong with the serpents? This is Mercury and he's connected to healing. This is why the first decans tend to be drawn to healing practices and the reason why they are more likely to be healthy.

The problem, however is that they can become hypochondriacs. Certain Virgos are obsessed with alternative therapies they become experts on arcane remedies and can provide the ideal health tips for everyoneeven people who are sick of listening to it.

The first decan type is highly adaptable , and many are left-handed, or the ambidextrous. They are hard-working and ambitious. They are a lot of fun and can become overly busy and neglect their health and relationships. Although they are not above manual work These types are more inclined to use their heads.

2. September through September 11,

Saturn is Saturn was the Roman god of agriculture, wealth time, dissolution, and wealth. His festival day, known as

Saturnalia was marked with banquets and gifts. This is also the source of our term "Saturday" originates. As he's also an important god that is associated with crucial lessons, this is also where we get the term "saturnine" in. Saturn is the god of this decan and thus explains many things.

People born in this decan are naturally organized and have a strong will and generally are unflappable. ideal instances of the British rigid face stereotype. Women of the second decan tend to be strong-set and extremely solid workers who are unable to grasp the concept of "no" and often even at the cost of their own health. Dry skin is also a tendency to be an issue, and requires the use of moisturizers.

These employees make great employees, provided that they have the potential for growth and advancement. If that's the case, those above are likely to be anxious. If her employer doesn't provide any of these, she'll not stay the duration of. It can cause many job-hopping with a lengthy resume of jobs with short-term duration that impress everyone.

Women born in this decade are obsessed with achievement as well as recognition and awards. They are extremely competitive often even to the point of being ruthless. Once they have reached the top of their game they are more likely to protect the people below them. The women of the zodiac sign generally make excellent bosses - great in their courtesy, delegating, and in encouraging employees.

They are perfectionists they expect to be treated the same way by others, both who are above and below them. This could lead to frustration sometimes and also to confusion and conflict with both superiors and subordinates.

The 2nd decan in Virgo also has an Capricorn sub-influence. It's not important what it is. What you should know is that this could create problems in a woman's life or career and turn her into an early blossomer.

That means that regardless of how hard they try however, they're unlikely to be able to achieve financial success until around the time they turn 30. After this point it's possible that things will improve however it's not likely that they'll be at the top until the end of their 50s or later.

This is an extremely risky moment. As they begin to see the results that their hard work is finally being rewarded, the fact that it will never be theirs due to so many obstacles could make them angry and cynical. They can also become aggressive. It's possible that long-term periods of depression and severe self-doubt may strike, and could have a negative effect on the people around them including relatives and friends.

The best method to tackle this is to realize that there's a limit to what one can accomplish. Capricorn's influence is capable of creating chaos however, if you can keep going (an inherent ability of Virgos) There are rewards at the end.

Third Decan Third Decan 23

The governing force is Venus as Goddess of Love. However, it does also have an Taurus sub-influence that can result in quite intriguing outcomes.

The Venus influence can produce women who are reserved, quiet or shy, and extremely uncomfortable around attention. It's a shame since they usually have smooth skin and well-balanced bodies, as well as sensual lips, as being pleasing singing and speaking voices.

They are also talented with an excellent ability to hear pitch, making music an ideal career. People who work in the field of music usually perform in the role of a backup singer or chorus -- whatever is necessary to avoid being getting noticed. Although they love beautiful outfits and clothes They prefer keeping things basic and minimal not too loud and gaudy.

They are easily affected by emotions, and can fall in love fast and then hurting at the same time. It's not always easy to discern this, however, due to their knack for squeezing things up. They aren't slack but. They possess an incredible amount of patience, and can withstand many criticisms as well as pressure and disappointment. However, it is possible to go way too far, particularly when it comes to abusive relationships.

They are not without limits and that's when the Taurus sub-influence enters. Bulls are not as impulsive as they are commonly depicted. In reality, they often require convincing to participating in the bull-fighting rings.

While Venus is patient and sensitive, Taurus has a steely determination and a fiery temper. When they're pushed to the limit the third decan woman can react, causing shock to not only themselves and others and even others. In this way, they are often passive aggressive by using silence and resoluteness as weapons until they eventually explode.

Although women born under this decan are able to have a flexible nature, they prefer regularity. Although they aren't usually adventurous but they can be extremely determined when they decide on something. In combination with their stubbornness and persistence, their methodical approach and the tendency of others to undervalue them (including them) they could go extremely far.

Chapter 6: The Cusps

The sun's crossing of two zodiac signs is the reason for those who believe they aren't the type of sign for them. Therefore, let's explore the personality types of these people.

the Leo-Virgo Cusp from August 19 through August 24

Leo's fiery flamboyance contrasts the calmness of Virgo and leads to exuberant raging types who enjoy periods of intense alone time. They are extremely effective communicators and possess excellent conversational and manipulative skills, which makes them great diplomats, lawyers salespersons, televangelists and salespeople.

They also enjoy playing the game. Together with their inherent social skills, determination as well as their persistence, focus on details, and quick wit they are usually great business people, as long as they are able to temper their love of the risk.

The women of the Leo-Virgo cusp are typically physically active, devoted to healthand meticulous about their diet and hygiene. They tend to prefer group sports in preference to solitary sports like running, and excel in managing teams -- a major advantage for those in business. The downside is that they may get caught on their appearance, and become a bit smug and shallow, just like the gym-goers and fashion-conscious victims.

Leo's influence makes them extremely aggressive and domineering But Virgo's influence could make them too sensitive and private. They will force men into going out, and then treat them like job seekers on the day of the date. People they like will not hear the phrase, but they will. They are sceptical of words, and would rather to show rather than tell.

The Virgo-Libra Cusp September 19 through September 24

Women born during this period are fascinated by beauty. They enjoy the arts as well as attractive people. They are great museum curators and art collectors. They're not the frenzied types but. The influence of Virgo is that they are grounded with an focus on the finer details and a keen focus on the organization.

The problem with this type The problem with this kind of person is that even though they are able to appreciate the beauty and talents of others however, they are not able to think creatively. They are able to explain what makes a work of art is amazing, but seldom create it for themselves. They're also health-conscious However, they run the risk of becoming hypochondriacs.

This desire for beauty may cause them to be insecure, compulsive, and obsessed with style and appearances. For those with small pockets this could be problematic. The Virgo-Libra cusp ladies can be extremely critical, seeing imperfections in everything, even their own. This is the kind of woman that pressures her children into achieving straight A's and insists that they become lawyers, doctors and engineers, constantly reminding them of the gruelling hours she endured in labor.

However, in general they are socially friendly, compassionate and romantic, committed and playful. Libra's influence makes them open-minded and extremely fair, which makes them excellent judges and diplomats. They are awestruck by conversation, adept at debates and are skilled at playing devil's advocatewhich is sometimes difficult for their families friends, lovers, and family members.

Chapter 7: General Advice

Being a Virgo isn't an easy task providing general advice to a sign that has multiple variations isn't feasible. However, there are certain threads that connect every type of Virgo women. If you take them with a pinch of salt and tailored to your personal circumstances, these suggestions can be a great help.

You are the obstacle you create yourself.

Life is already hard enough If you're faced with an angelic celestial virgin telling your to keep your distance this can make it even more difficult. Your signification is rigid, and that's why your planet is earth. This is why you prefer to prioritize obligations and duty over your personal happiness as well as your job and routines over your life.

The world isn't all black and white.

Do not forget the fact that you've been taught to believe in a different world. The world isn't perfect , and regardless of how you try you can't make it perfect. It's the imperfections and unpredictable nature and uncertainty of our world which makes it such an interesting living space however, you must be willing to accept the world in the way it is and not the way you would like it to be.

It's okay to express opinions or criticize We are each entitled to the opinions of others. However, don't let this stop you from interacting with other people or taking on new interests simply because society doesn't like it. You are entitled to be weird, bizarre or even different in the sense that you wish to be.

Step up

It's a known fact that Virgo women tend to stay in positions or jobs they're not qualified for. It is due to their love of appearances, perfection and order. Even if you're competent for a higher level position, you're scared that you'll fail, and everybody will be aware. You settle for a junior-level position rather, because it will make you appear flawless.

When it comes to relationships Virgo females tend to remain with males (or any other females) regardless of whether there's nothing sparking in it. It's because they enjoy routines, fear what other people think of them or feel that there's no one who is like their needs. If you don't realize that happiness lies with you and the choices you make, and not with the opinions of other people the rest of your life is likely to be boring.

In their work or in their private life, Virgo women tend to be patiently waiting for the perfect time. This is in line with their notion of a hierarchical, structured world which is that if they try for long enough and are persistent enough, the perfect moment will be thrown at them.

It's unlikely to ever happen. That's why a frequent complaint from Virgo women is the feeling that they're not living their lives to their fullest.

As as a Virgo As a Virgo, you're caught between the mercurial and virginal. The former will keep you secure, grounded, and secure. Let the latter guide you and motivate you to take action.

How to Attract a Virgin

If you're looking ways of attracting women born between the 23rd of August between August 23rd and September 22nd, you should go through the following article. It will give you some strategies on how and when to attract her. Additionally, you'll learn the best ways to do to make sure to get her attention at every move that you take. In addition, you'll receive the guidelines of the things you must do and shouldn't do if you intend to keep that type of friendship with her. It is essential to follow every step to ensure that you will be able to identify the loopholes out and treat her as she would like to be treated.

Make Friendship a priority as The First Step

The most effective way one could describe the characteristics of a Virgo female is to say that she likes to learn about what she is interested in more. That means that if you want to impress her, you must put in more effort into getting her to be a friend. Allow her to have the space she requires to ensure that she gets to get to know you more intimately. Do not hurry into a sexual relationship with her or sharing sexual desires on the very first day of your date. This is a sure way to ensure that you will not succeed in wooing her. Make sure that you give her time as well as space she requires to allow you to understand her more, and once she's gained confidence in you, you're sure to win her over.

You must always make the Steps First

Another description you should keep in mind is that you're likely to encounter an introverted person. In general, girls in the Virgo are shy. If you're looking to develop a relationship with her, you have to be the first to move every time. If you're looking to build a an intimate relationship with her, then you need to step outside into your own comfort zone. inform her exactly what you want to tell her. There are many people who fail when trying to get these girls' attention quit thinking they're not interested.

While you're making the transitions when you make the moves, keep these tips in your head:

* Always be confident in what you do. The Virgo woman loves men who are confident and confident in every move that he takes. For example, if you are planning to go out with her make sure you are exact, clear, and confident when asking her. You'll be surprised at how many times she'll be enticed to join you.

* You must make sure that everything you do is as traditional , in that you do not have be able to demonstrate a high level of expertise in a specific area. Remember that Virgo women are introverted.

Be romantically soft with her

When you are trying to make moves and try to win her over it is important to make use of soft, romantic phrases towards her because it will result in winning the hearts of most Virgo women. In other words, instead of using the term hot to describe her appearance, you must always use the word beautiful. Always remember that if you're going to succeed in winning her love, you must be steady and consistent in all that you do. There is no need to play games with an Virgo woman. The games are not the only thing she wants from a lover. In all situations you must be kind and loving to her. She requires a gentle love that can give her the confidence that everything is going well and helps ease some of her anxieties.

Maintain A Superior Intensity

There are many descriptions of the type of person the Virgo seeks however if you're not a very intelligent person, the things will not go well for you. You must have a certain degree of intelligence to keep her brain busy with the issues that impact people's lives discuss social events and other topics you can talk about with her. A majority of Virgo women are well-informed about the majority of things that they are concerned about. about the topics you can think of.

Take a look at Her Feelings

It is also crucial that you are capable of discerning her mood while you are together. Sometimes, they are insecure enough to not make a move , so you must assume the responsibility to observe her gaze. Learn what she is looking for when she performs certain actions to draw your attention. It is not a good idea to be someone who is spending the majority of the time not paying attention to certain gestures she makes as she might become very bored and , being an animal, you might have a difficult time trying to manage her these moments.

Put Your Money Into The Way You Dress

It is a fact that if you're hoping to make it to the scene of romance with the sign of a Virgo then you should dress up. It's not normal dress code and it doesn't mean that you have to spend much on dressing. It is enough to be creative with the clothes you wear. If you aren't convinced this is the case, just look at the way the Virgo women dress, and you will see a creativeness in their attire. If they are able to dress this way, then why aren't you able to emulate?

Make sure you pay attention on your hygiene

You may have the most elegant clothes, but if don't pay attention to your hygiene standards, you need to take a step back of ever getting a Virgo woman. She is always seeking ways to keep you neat and tidy. So, it is important to be more attentive to the scent you emit as well as the cleanliness of your nose , and not forgetting about the looks at your eyes. The cleanliness of your home is not only on a personal basis and an Virgo woman wants to see a quality of order at home so don't be afraid to do your chores every day in case you end up losing her to a neat guy that is interested in her.

If you're ever hoping to impress her, then you must go to her home and observe the level of order can be found in the apartment. If you can achieve this, you should have an example for you to follow because you need to show the same degree of neatness or perhaps more. You don't want your wife to wake each day and go into your home and organize items for you. Women of the Virgo sign are able to do this, but the most important thing you should think about is how long she will accept this type of lifestyle. Make it a routine to take care of your clothes, put greater importance to the things she likes to view in your home because she is a lover of everything! If you can keep all this in your mind, you'll be confident of winning the Virgo.

Be A Whole Person

If you're looking for more details about the characteristics of a Virgo then you must be all things. Everything, in the sense that you need to have everything you need to keep her busy, engaged and always ready to engage in conversation. Most of the time, being smart can be a distraction from the other traits that are built and again, don't be too smart to ignore the social aspects women require. In essence, you must keep her brain active constantly keeping her delighted and interested at all times.

Help Her Reset

The mental state of the Virgo will be constantly in motion. If she's not stressed, then she's contemplating something. If you're going be able to make it work for her, then you have to have lots of patience. You also need to be very accommodating in dealing with her. Sometimes she might simply sit and not say anything whatsoever. There is no need to push or force her to speak. Just be patient and let her speak. It could be that she is looking for just a few things, and everything will be fine.

Be Honest and Punctual

One thing you must be certain to keep in mind when attracted to someone who is a Virgo will be to remain honest and to always adhere to your word. This is because the Virgo woman is a reliable person. You don't want to wait around for an appointment as it will most likely be negative. You must always establish an habit of keeping track of the time for each action you make. It is important to remember that you shouldn't expect to be always open about specific topics, let her be!

Dos and Don'ts If You'd Like To Be a Winner A Virgo

* You should demonstrate that you have a honest character when you're trying to impress her. Furthermore you must increase your trust to a point that she's more forthcoming about issues with you.

* You must be cautious not to make a show of boasting or trying to impress her by using money. This is because they aren't attracted by money, but by the character you possess and how you portray. Instead of spending a large amount of your money, put it aside until you become an active participant with humor, and you should ensure that you live a good life.

If you've determined to marry the Virgo and you've decided to do it, you should be delicate in how you interact with your

Virgo girlfriend. They are looking for gentlemen as they reflect the type of personality many women are searching for. Being timid does not mean that they are looking for someone who will enter their lives and be in control of everything and every aspect of their lives.

* If you're looking for the best method of winning over a woman of the Virgo sign, then the first thing you need to do is be aware of the things they are most passionate about. Do you want to try the scent of candles, they can be a bit mad. If you don't think this is enough then maintain the scent of fresh laundry. They love the scent of well-chosen perfumes.

* If you've been trying to get rid of women who aren't willing to forgive even when you don't intend to harm them, then you ought to test out the sign of Virgo. They are able to forgive you, especially when they learn that you really regret it however, you must be careful not to repeat the hurt they caused you.

* You must always be sure to fulfill the promises you make when you plan to be

the lottery as a Virgo. It is not a good idea to leave a woman waiting for a commitment that you are unable to keep, as it will allow you to have the chance to end in a position where you don't want to be in. You must keep every promise you make.

* Always be neat and refrain from making your clothes filthy because this can have some detrimental negative effects when you're with the Virgo.

So, if you're in the market and trying to figure out how to win the love of the Virgo woman, you must to get outside of your comfortable zone and show her that you can accomplish the most extraordinary. Show her the respect she deserves, and always be grateful for her efforts. There is nothing better for her than a spouse who has her best interests in mind. Always consider it as your goal for her to demonstrate the love she deserves. You must be extremely consistent in all that you do, and most importantly be able to understand her. If you do this, you'll be able to enjoy relationships and moving it to the next level of dating.

Dating A Virgo Woman

Before you make that big step to make it a point to take your relationship with an Virgo up a notch, you need to be conversant of the various steps you must take to ensure that it works. You must fully be aware of the most important things you must know about dating. If you're looking to date an Virgo You should be aware that dating is completely unique due to the traits that are associated with the woman are unique and unique. It is important to realize that you're not dating a shy lady, but also one seeking the perfectionist. If you're looking to find a partner, then you'll need to follow these tips.

She Loves Working

If you're looking for someone who will sit back and relax at home , this is your chance to relax and unwind. A Virgo woman excels at her job to the highest level. She enjoys being self-sufficient throughout the day. They are highly productive, never resting since they're always prepared to go to work. It does not matter what type of job they work in, as long as they can earn a decent living, it is important to know the types of jobs that are suitable for Virgo women.

It's all about comfort.

There are people who enjoy doing many things, and have different preferences when it comes to certain choices. For example, there are people who are fond than just dressing, but at the cost of making their surroundings feel comfortable. If you're a woman of the Virgo sign you'll get the opportunity to meet one who is extremely comfortable in all she does. So, if you're searching for methods and ways to date, you must ensure that she is comfortable every day.

Be Careful when dealing with money

For many years, women have been viewed as a good choice in the world of shopping. However, if seeking that woman who is passionate about making use of the small or huge amount of money she has , you should be dating the Virgo woman. So, if you're looking for a lady that will enter your life and organize your financial requirements that you have to meet take a leap of faith to meet the Virgo. They'll advise that you go above and beyond your typical spending and take advantage of every chance they get to make purchases using coupons they receive. They are also adept in utilizing sales that you could receive.

Education is the key

If you're dating a Virgo woman, it is important to keep in mind the fact that she's a believer in education. Education is her primary factor in a successful life. Therefore, you could see her constantly having that involve research, writing, and reading. Always try to help her through this type of situation when she exhibits indicators of schooling.

Best Jobs for Virgos

If you're searching for the perfect job for those born between August 23rd and September 22nd , then you must know what sort of job to search for by reading this article. It is also an aid to those seeking jobs and are in the range of Virgos. Based on the personalities displayed by these personalities, you are sure to find the most effective employee who is always hardworking and eager to do things in the correct way. Based on his or her structured behavior you will be sure of getting the most out of the Virgo.

If you're an Virgo and you are searching to find the ideal job, then you should consider steady work. This is due to the fact that Virgos tend to not be very impulsive, and they are not prone to doing all the things at once. In fact, they are inclined to focus and settle down on the work they are already doing. If you're an employee searching for a worker who will ensure that the goals of your business are achieved and that the company's rules are followed, Then you must look for the sign of a Virgo.

The process of instructing others to do the work is crucial for the Virgo. If you are the services of a Virgo then it is important to constantly emphasize the areas where you require them to place more focus. In this way, you'll receive the most effective outcomes from the Virgo. In case this isn't enough, if you're looking for changes to instructions, then you have to communicate clearly with them. You must prepare ahead so that they will have the motivation to remain vigilant.

Tax Auditor General

Because Virgos are well-known for being very critical of the things they do, you must take them through your financial records while they revise them. The majority of people wouldn't choose to do this as they might encounter others. For those who are Virgo this is a chance to put up a new precedent and put everything in writing. Because they are extremely superior and love to feel fulfilled when doing things in the right way, regardless of the outcome you can trust their expertise in these kinds of job.

Nutritional Expert

The subject of nutrition is one that is not something you want to make fun of. Virgos are recognized as being very natural in all ways which is why they have a heart for helping people and the desire to help a lot of people that might need their help. Because they're adept in managing their health you can rest assured that you'll receive the most qualified nutritionist if you decide to work with any of their services. They're not just the ones who promote water and wine. They take their work seriously , to the point where they can provide the top individuals to work with.

House Cleaner

One characteristic that can be described as the Virgo is their love to make everything tidy. So if you're searching for the ideal cleaner for your home, consider thinking about calling one as they will provide you with provide the house assistance you require. One thing to take the time to do is and implement changes to your home. Remember that they are clean people, and your home and you will remain tidy for the duration of time you keep them in your house.

The Most Effective Assistant

You are able to test all the different assistants that you can choose from however once you've made your choice or have the opportunity to acquire a Virgo then you've hit the jackpot. These are the kinds of people you'll need at home, in your workplace and at your business. If you're asking yourself what exactly you want from consider taking time to consider the traits you want in the assistant you'll need. One of the traits you're looking for is someone who is organized and enthusiastic about what they are doing. This is why you require an Virgo as your assistant because you can find one who won't be irritated when you assign the burden of many responsibilities. It is essential to have an assistant who is organized and who is able to hold the items that you require or become sloppy with the appointments you've created. If you are the type of person you're seeking, then do not be afraid to choose an assistant named Virgo.

The Most Professional Archivist You Can Find

Sorting things is among the skills you must have to consider when searching for an archive specialist. You require someone who will find all the items you want to keep in your archive and organize them in a manner that it is easy to access the items. This is among the traits you need to seek out. If you are able to identify this type of character and add the organized mind, you will find that the Virgo is the right fit for your company and you. It is certain that you will get someone who will work with dedication and in a positive manner. They appreciate the job they are doing more than the pay they earn since they enjoy working in a comfortable environment.

Technician

If you're looking for the most effective technician you can find, then you should consider the possibility of the Virgo. They excel at conducting research and accumulating the data will help you make the best decisions you'll need following a thorough review of the collected, verified and compared information.

The nature of the Astrological signs

What's the meaning behind your symbol? His past? His qualities?

Like all people has an astrological signification based on the date you were born. The astrological sign you choose to follow can reveal much about your personality, personal characteristics, your preferences and even your motives. This Book will show you the qualities of the twelve zodiac signs with respect to Virgo Discover all the aspects to know your astrological sign!

The Virgin: The third sign of summer, feminine changeable Earth that is controlled by Mercury.

Mythology: These were virgin goddesses, such as Athena or Hestia goddess of home, and particularly Demeter or Ceres, goddess of motherhood, of the earth as well as of the harvests, sister to Zeus.

Character and symbolism Character and symbolism: In the zodiac, Virgo is a symbol of analysis methods, measurement, organization, classification. He is a rational and hardworking practical, supportive and self-aware meticulous mind. Insecure, he displays timidity and shields himself from any type of intrusion The goal is preservation and safety. This is a sign that is connected to health, medicine eating habits, hygiene, and diet. A maniac, he is frequently obsessed with household chores and chores of the day. Innovative and technically skilled He puts his skills to good use for other people.

In love with orderly manner of doing things, he prefers things to be carried out in accordance with the rules of art, yet he has his own rules are his own. He is the king of criticism and advice. This type of personality is a bit snobby always with the last word, and can often upset people around him because of being better than everybody else. But, his kindness makes him indispensable , and his practicality can be a boon when faced with any challenge.

He's afflicted with a confidence deficit and is often himself in the shadows by people who have the confidence to stand up for themselves. Her modesty isn't always helping her.

Insecure, discontented and rigid, he's an anxious individual who has a difficult time expressing his feelings. He is hidden behind a mask of control and coldness that is difficult to let go of. The Virgin is a person who has problems let go. When she is stressed, she is stiffer and even more self-critical and perfectionist: His expectations of his own self are huge.

Affirmed, he will give up his time for the people who he cherishes and give all he has to offer without complaint the native of Virgo is never happier than when he realizes the value of his work!

He is usually discreet, but he could transform into a true pipette and share the latest gossip.

When it comes to love, this sign is a bit stoic, critical and not all that romantic. He is trying to control his feelings and all that is human in him, including the emotional side. Self-conscious, shy, and unsure He has a deep fear of being disregarded. But, when it does happen without inhibitions and self-consciousness, the"wise" Virgo transforms into a maniacal Virgo and begins to be sexually wild but there is always the need to maintain on top of things. As a sign that indicates celibacy and a tendency to be a single person, as it allows him to be independent. If Virgo decides to marry to be comfortable, it's for the sake of comfort or to satisfy a need.

Keywords: Purification, chastity, analysis, criticism, order, reason, division, doubt, subtraction, limitation, reserve, practice, method, detail, egoism, service, work, technique, medicine, virginity, mania, precision.

Famous Virgins : Agatha Christie - Greta Garbo - Sophia Loren Irene Joliot-Curie - Beyonce - Cameron Diaz - Mylene Farmer Mother Teresa - Segolene Royal - Amy Winehouse - Adriana Karembeu - Claudia Schiffer - Salma Hayek - Raquel Welch Elisabeth Ire d ' England.

Richelieu Louis XIV - Guillaume Apollinaire Michel Drucker Chateaubriand Goethe -- Richard Gere - Michael Jackson Ronsard

The cast includes Freddie Mercury - Keanu Reeves Keanu Reeves Sean Connery - Henry of Wales Stephen King - Tim Burton.

Affinity signs with the Virgin : Taurus and the Capricorn and the Cancer Scorpion, and the Scorpion.

The most troublesome signs associated with Virgo: Sagittarius, Gemini. Another sign associated with Virgo is the Fish.

If the Virgin was:

The color is one: Yellow-green beige and gray.

Metals: Mercury

* A stone: Jasper, Tourmaline, Agate.

* A creature The ant, bees and animals of the farmyard. * A plant: Cereals, lavender.

* A mineral: Nickel

* A part of the body The intestines.

* One country: Brazil, Turkey, West Indies, United States,

The former Yugoslavia, Crete, Mesopotamia, Lower Silesia, State of Virginia.

* A profession: Doctor, nurse, pharmacist, accountant, surveyor, veterinarian, herbalist, expert.

* One day in the week Wednesday

* One number: 10 15, 27,

Note to the reader: Fa

The image depicts the Virgo woman

It is said that the Virgo woman is meticulous and discreet. She is very nice with whom to spend time. She has a keen sense of order and responsibility.

The native can't think about leaving her job without everything being neat and perfect. She also feels very at ease in the social world and knows how to express her enthusiasm. However, the native is naturally anxious. She is usually worried about doing something wrong and not providing complete satisfaction to her family and friends and of feeling abandoned or not loved.

The Virgo woman is drawn to the bright, she is known for organizing a large occasion, but is a bit in the background during the event. She may also possess an occasional lesson-giving aspect which irritates her. This is not a deliberate act and if anyone is able to point it out to her, she'll likely be extremely embarrassing and will want to rectify the situation quickly.

Since the Virgo woman is blessed with qualities for heart, which are irresistible and unquestionable, she will not harm the fly, and she would rather than anything to feel valued. She isn't averse to making decisions and thinks through her decisions before taking action.

The Virgo woman as well as the males

For her the world is all black. The fragility and sadness that characterize the Virgo woman can enthral men or even annoy them! For some, she is the ideal woman. For some, she's too anxious and sensitive which is why she's associated with long boring conversations.

In any case, her lovers will do any kind of thing for her and she's not afraid to make use of it. However, the Virgo woman isn't rude and she sets the boundaries of her own.

Her main issue is that she is prone to be attracted to men who aren't interested in her or seem too far away for her.

The Virgo woman is in need of a true connection, love and attention. When she's in love, she can be very possessive. She would love to turn into a Don Juan into a frozen lover. Naturally, this doesn't work, and the native now in all shapes, forms, doubts, and hundreds of questions. To be content in relationship the Virgo woman must surely to alter her behavior and examine her priorities. It could be that happiness is within his reach.

The persona is that of the Virgo man

The Virgo man is a person with a strong sense of duty. He is a good servant and is practical.

The concern for safety and his fear of the future makes him a diligent worker who doesn't do his job at hand.

He is demanding and loves not to be apprehensive or spending his time. He'll do whatever it takes to arrange his life so that there's never an obstacle in his way.

This characteristic hinders him from pursuing his dreams He would like to travel and discover new perspectives, but he prefers the comforts of home and his familiar routines.

It is said that the Virgo man is trustworthy and considerate of others and does not wish to hurt anyone or harm them in any manner. As with his female counterparts he isn't one to be seen as a sexy person with the possibility of being too quiet.

The Virgo man appears to be at first, extremely dependent on order and established rules. However it is possible to be extremely tolerant with regards to the people who are around him. The bonds of friendship and social connections which he makes are in actual fact, extremely important for him.

Women and men of the Virgo sign

In love in love, in love, the Virgo man is charming, gentle and extremely polite.

He's never abrupt, or obnoxious, and due to his sensitive nature, he is able to detect what women are thinking. He is shy and won't ever meet women when he isn't confident and secure.

He's in search of an honest and steady person similar to his. The way he is sensitive differs from many men. This could make him vulnerable, however, it also provides him with an innate elegance and ability to be in the shoes of someone else.

The native is charming however, he is difficult to satisfy. When he's feeling love He doesn't attempt to control his lover and lets her move about whenever she wants.

On the other hand, he also needs the utmost sincerity, comfort, and time with family. That's where his equilibrium lies. The Virgo man is determined to live the rest of his time with the exact same lady. He is loyal sincere and honest, but he is not a women's man. He's not seeking the ultimate victory but instead for the stability.

Virgo, Earth sign, is the sixth zodiac sign and is controlled by Mercury and all that Mercury represents exchanges. The exchanges Virgo is already doing with her own self, constantly pondering whether she is an unrefined spirit or simply be a spirit. She is unbeatable in taking into consideration the benefits and disadvantages. This can go on for several hours. What an ego!

The woman who is virgo Salma Hayek is a virgo Man virgo

HUGH GRANT is the Virgo

Your Love Compatibility

Virgo woman & Virgo man

Don't be fooled by two people with the same name will always are able to get along because they ought to be able to communicate with each other.

It is believed that the Virgo woman and man Virgo woman However, they have a good chance of meeting. "Agreement" can be the key to qualifying. In reality, Virgos are right, quiet, and courteous It's not in this kind of couple that we'll go to theater in which offensive words are exchanged.

However the opposite is that these couples often lack enthusiasm and enthusiasm The relationship may be a breeze, but it may lack emotion and warmth. They are primarily attached to protection and the material items. This blend lacks imagination or spontaneity. The parties may want to remain in a more secluded way and not be the ones to initiate meetings.

If they don't put in the efforts to separate themselves from the world and their surroundings, they'll soon become bored. They'll be warm and comfortable, and they'll be able to return as often as they can.

To break out of the monotony that may be felt by others, a strong desire for a shared goal must unite the two people who are ours. However, their bond regardless of how sane it might be, will be a source of joy for them. If they don't try to be a part of their current life, they'll become bored.

The homes they will share are warm they will feel comfortable and provide as much as is possible. To break out of what may seem boring to certain people, a deep passion for a common ideal must unite our two neighbors. Their friendship no matter how peaceful it may be, could bring them joy. If they don't take the time to get away from the world around them, they'll eventually become bored.

To escape what may appear to some as boring, a huge desire for a common goal is required brought our two natives together. Their relationship regardless of how calm it might be, may suffice to make them extremely happy.

How do you seduce based on the signs of the astrology?

Which one is best for you?

Astrology can aid you to attract the person you want to be with It is just a matter of know the way it is working and how it wants to be treated and seduced. Astro.fr offers you the secrets to seduction. No sign will resist!

(Aries (From 23 March until April 20)

Compatibility in love Virgo, Aries

What do you love about the Aries his determination, energy and determination, his magnetic speed, his creativity and his honesty.

What's the secret to its success? It is certain that Aries will make you push yourself to go where you're afraid to go. For you can tell, you'll be able to calm and stabilize it. The relationship you have with your partner is therefore possible but it will take much effort.

What causes it to not work It is that you will face lots of problems living as in an Aries who is too emotional and angered. Furthermore, you'll find the person as too angry and, conversely when he sees you as too shyand reserved There is a very low chances that it will succeed!

Sex-Erotic Compatibility: There's nothing in common , and other than a wild and sexy Virgo It won't work!

It is believed that Aries will be the most energetic symbol of the Zodiac which is exactly what happens in his relationship! He is more attracted by quick and intense pleasures than long-running foreplay sessions, then and then the main course as well as sweets ...

* The Aries are not happy being denied his passion, therefore you must allow him to indulge in his wild desires before you can be touched however, when the Aries is happy, he'll show to be tender and loving to make wishes.

To keep him interested you must learn to manage his passion as well as letting him believe that he's at the helm of circumstances. It's a difficult game for novices but it is vital to the health of your loved ones. If you can limit his appetite and not cause him to explode whenever you get the urge and you'll be an impressive Aries!

* Signs for which Aries has the highest compatible erotic aspects:

* Aries man: Aries, Gemini, Libra

* Aries woman: Aries, Gemini, Libra, Pisces

The astrological signs can aid you in understanding the person in order to attract her. Find out the secrets that the Aries sign has to offer as well as the ways he prefers to be wooed and embraced and this Aries can't be in a position to resist you!

The Aries are the most impulsive of people who tend to be quick to the right. There is no need to sit long with them. your attraction will determine the extent of the chemistry you share. Don't be afraid to turn down an Aries since he may interpret it as a snub or even as an opportunity!

If you're looking to start an ongoing relationship, you'll need to attract his attention or even provoke it to lure him into your webs. It is the most difficult thing to do is to convince him that it's always he is the one who dances!

Aries, you and your astral love compatibility

Aries, Astrology can assist you to know other signs of astrology and help you be aware of which ones you are most at ease with and with whom you're most likely to get your relationship working. Aries Are you prepared to learn which zodiac sign works best for you?

Aries(From March 21 until April 20)

The fiery disposition of Aries works well with fire signs specifically like Aries , Leo and Sagittarius as they are in the same boat and the passion that drives the three can spark beautiful flames. A small flat for Sagittarius who might not be able to find the romantic declarations of love that they are so fond of, since the Aries is not a very social person and would rather to express his feelingsrather than give long passionate speeches .

The signs of the air, Gemini , Libra and Aquarius are all likely to have an amazing complementarity with Aries in the sense that the latter's energy can be stimulating to start projects for two people and break out of the routine that hinders the signs of air. It is therefore likely that passion will be in the air however beware of slippages that can lead to a bitter angry resentment!

When you consider the earth signs: Taurus , Virgo and Capricorn The understanding is less certain as these signs require patience and stability, while Aries frequently acts on impulse and with a high degree of spontaneity. The relationship may be able to last in the event that the Aries is able to connect and be vulnerable however, you must be aware that the Aries is not a fan of compromise, even when they appear feasible at first ...

However in the case of the water signs of Cancer , Scorpio and Pisces relationships can be a challenge for the long haul! Even though the beginnings appear promising, particularly under the cover, once the passion is gone and the essence the signs of each will come back in a hurry and display the difference in their expectations that at least one of the two (if not both) will end up very disappointed!

Virgo Love, your astral and compatibility (From August 23 through September 22)

The Virgin may display great feelings of ambivalence regarding his sexuality and, if it is a natural trait it is an introverted personality it could be as passionate like the woman who is harpy. In other words, you could be in a relationship with a completely different person. It will be largely dependent on the level of sexual attraction which will be abound between you.

It usually takes some time before you notice her breaking free of the chains that she has imposed on her, however, she will quickly turn fiery and leave you stunned at the sight of her incredible energy.

It's normal to want to be pleasing Virgo So it's your job to discover the locks that cause her to shiver. Be aware, however, that should she be disappointed by your behavior, she'll get a grip on herself.

Signs that Virgo has the highest compatible erotic relationship: Virgo man: Taurus, Cancer, Leo, Virgo Capricorn Pisces

Virgo woman: Taurus, Virgo, Libra, Scorpio, Capricorn, Aquarius

How do you seduce the attention of a Virgo?

The astrological signs can help you to understand the person in order to attract her. Learn about the Virgo sign is hiding, how they prefer to be wooed and embraced and this Virgo will be unable to be averse to you!

Virgin (From August 23rd until September 22)

The Virgin you may appear to be a bit stiff and difficult to approach However, underneath his icy exterior is a persona ready to explode! If you are able to create love between you and Virgo, Virgo is likely to lose control and loosen up, and give you the best they can offer.

Therefore, it is up to you to constantly animate this spark to ensure that the Virgin doesn't diminish in her intensity. Be aware that she is highly receptive to positive assertions, but on contrary, she is averse to excellent talkers.

Virgo Love your astral self compatibility

Virgo, Astrology can help you comprehend other astrological signs and help you determine which zodiac signs you're most compatible and with which signs you are most likely to find your love affair flourish. Virgo Are you prepared to learn what other zodiac sign is suitable for you?

Virgin (From August 23rd until September 22)

In the other signs of the earth (Taurus, Virgo, Capricorn) In the other signs (Taurus, Virgo, Capricorn), you are completely out of the perspective, and also in your shared desire to create positive plans for the future. Your rationality is your driving force and you are able to be in a happy and long-lasting relationship, if your routine can be broken.

The water signs (Cancer, Scorpio, Pisces) could provide Virgo the evidence of love that they require to feel safe within their relationships. The relationship won't be a passionate one, but that is not the type of relationship Virgo is looking for, and prefers complicity and comfort. Thus, they will grow with confidence and satisfaction.

The Virgin is enthralled by the unending power associated with the three fire signs (Aries, Leo and Sagittarius) however, it will not require a long time to sail! However, a bit of angst could make a slightly prescient Virgo quite a bit of good. The signs of fire don't offer her the security she desires However, she may become too cautious and be a victim of this disrespect.

The signs of the air (Gemini, Libra, Aquarius) are a real challenge for you! They are lighthearted, and it is a pain to need to search for evidence of affection. The relationship could work in the event that you are a tiger sign ascendant and are willing acknowledge their need to be free. Great for couples with short lengths however, never too lengthy ...

Compatibility in love Virgo, Virgo

What is it that pleases you about the Virgin Her manner of conduct Her depth of thought Her calm and rational side and her integrity of thought.

What makes it work? In the same way You are very similar in your ideas and the principles of living, which could draw you closer. Therefore, you share the same goals, the identical goals and your relationships could be very well-balanced.

What is the reason it doesn't work is that you are drawn to the creature and keep teasing yourself. In the end your relationship may be ruined. It's your responsibility to be less demanding and critical!

Sex-erotic compatibility: "It's possible to be done' according to the saying, even if you have the option of alternating intervals of passion and wisdom.

(Taurus (From to April 21, until May 20)

Compatibility of love Virgo, Taurus

What do you love most about Taurus Its comforting and calm nature. His sense of sensitivity, his love of life well-balanced humor, and the tone of his voice.

What is it that makes it work? Since both are Earth signposts, it's formed from the same mold and get along as thieves. All the elements are in place to create a harmonious couple.

What is the reason it doesn't work? The only issue is most likely to be the absence of communication or exchange However, you'll always be able to reach a common understanding and
listen. Allow the time and time of your life happen.

Sex-Erotic Compatibility: Although you may not have the identical expectations, you remain on the same page.

* The Taurus enjoys sex and the pleasure is found in the sex. He'll probably be more hesitant to engage in foreplay , however he will be able to please your desires without a problem throughout the night because his commitment to you will be exemplary.

He's not averse to kisses during the process and may be extremely happy If you take initiative during your romance however, on the other hand when you do not accept him or don't let him fulfill the desires of his heart, he could abandon you.

We all know that the Taurus is extremely affluent Therefore, if you intend to leave you will be hurting him to the maximum extent however, if you are willing to give all of yourself to him, he'll surely be able to turn you into an incredibly sexually satisfied person.

Signs for which Taurus is the most relationship with erotics:

Taurus man : Taurus, Virgo, Libra, Sagittarius, Pisces Taurus woman: Taurus, Virgo, Scorpio, Pisces

How do you charm an Taurus?

The astrological signification will help you identify the one you are looking to attract her. Learn about the Taurus sign is hiding, as well as its way of wanting to be wooed and embraced and this Taurus isn't going to be capable of resisting you!

Taurus

Taurus (From 22nd April until May 20)

The Taurus is usually extremely tactile, he loves affectionate hugs and melee. So when you are looking to seduce him, there's nothing simpler, all you need to do is to be ready to play! Naturally, a little resistance from your side will enhance your relationship and draw his attention. Taurus is a very shrewd and intelligent sign. Taurus is also extremely egocentric and you should be careful not to play around with the Taurus too much on the subject, or else you run the risk of watching him completely distance himself from you.

Also, be aware that Taurus likes stories that are long and he loves hesitant beginnings, brimming with mutual passion which is why he will be annoyed by excessive impatience from your side.

Taurus Your astral love compatibility

Astrology for Taurus can help you to know other signs of astrology and help you be aware of which zodiac signs you're most compatible with , and with whom you're most likely to get your relationship blossom. Taurus Are you willing to learn which zodiac sign is the best one for you?

Taurus (From 22nd April through May 20) Taurus (April 21 to May 20) Taurus is naturally drawn to the water indications (Cancer, Scorpio, Pisces) because his needs for love will be recognized by those extremely generous and sensual signs. The relationship between them can become very intimate if they have a common interest and are sincere with one another. in which case, Taurus's demands will be fulfilled!

A lovely bond could be formed between those born under the Earth sign (Taurus, Virgo and Capricorn) as they have the same goals and hopes in the near future! However, the issue could stem due to their relationship with money, and also from the investments that they each intend to do on their own in their area, rather than sharing the investment with each others. So long as the communication is going on that level, the issue won't be an issue!

The sign of fire (Aries , Leo and Sagittarius), Taurus will be more than a bit troubled because the constantly changing requirements of fire signs significantly alter their core nature which longs for more peace! To make the relationship sustainable for the

Taurus, the Taurus must use his dynamism to continuously delight his lover or the fire signs reduce their wanderlust, which isn't a given!

There is no cordial relationship with the Air signs (Gemini, Libra and Aquarius) but a bond built on compromises, in which each of them is trying to put their own needs ahead that of their counterparts. The Taurean's egocentricity will cause a stumbling block for the air signs who need to be free of any restrictions. The Taurus are prone to not feeling loved in the way they desire.

(Gemini (From to May 21, until June 20)

The love compatibility Virgo, Gemini

What do you find appealing about Gemini The openness of his mind as well as his desire for innovation as well as his unique ability to analyze and adaptability and gestures, as well as his language.

What is the reason it works: As both are ruled by Mercury the the planet that deals in exchange, both will have a good relationship and can boost projects and initiatives.

What is the reason it doesn't work is that you don't communicate with the same frequency and will frequently encounter disagreements. Additionally to this, the Gemini sign will see you as too rigid and you will become disappeared. There's no chance it will succeed!

Sex-erotic compatibility: Without having excessive expectations. you'll not be truly dissatisfied, but you might not share the same goals.

Gemini is a sign of freedom. Gemini is a sprightly indication that it doesn't need limitations, and that's the reason the Gemini is a lover of love, in all forms any form! He is a lover of experimentation but would rather enjoy a good classical, he is not averse to domineering tendencies, but is a fan of being dominated ...

The key element will lie in the character of his companion, who should be as open and generous as he is, or else, the Gemini may feel trapped by an uninteresting routine which he hates.

Imagine is the motor that drives him, so if you utilize and abuse your creativity and he'll be attracted to you the more. The more you challenge your mind and stimulate his mind, the more he'll be rewarded!

Signs that Gemini has the highest compatible erotic relationship: Gemini man: Aries, Gemini, Leo, Sagittarius

Gemini woman: Aries, Gemini, Leo, Libra, Sagittarius

How can you charm Geminis? Gemini?

A natal sign from the astrology can help you to understand the person you are looking to lure her. Learn about exactly what Gemini sign has to offer as well as how it would like to be wooed and embraced and this Gemini is not in a position to resist!

Gemini (From to May 21, until June 20)

The Gemini likes to talk and transmit information, and to learn about the preferences of everyone, it's an easy task to charm him , especially if you possess an impressive vocabulary. He'll expect total commitment from you, and will not comprehend complicated personalitiesthat are filled with self-consciousness and the appearance of modesty.

There is a greater chance to impress him during the evening since he's an individual with a highly active social life, and is a party animal. However you'll always need to come up with something that will keep your conversations going and to arouse the interest of him so that he doesn't get bored of you and drifts away to more attractive people.

Gemini and your astral love compatibility

Gemini, Astrology can help you to know other signs of astrology and help you determine which signs you're most at ease with and with which signs you are most likely to find your relationship flourish. Gemini Are you prepared to learn which zodiac sign is the best one for you?

Gemini (From the 21st of May until June 20)

Signs of fire (Aries, Leo and Sagittarius) can create an intense and passionate relationship with Gemini since they have a strong need for exploration and constant actions in their relationships. Gemini are a dynamic and energetic sign. Gemini are prone to express themselves physically and verbally as fire sign are adept at channeling this powerful flow of energy. The Gemini who is calmer needs to be more seductive and brave enough to face these extravagant fire signs with a desire for thrills.

The Air signs (Gemini, Libra, Aquarius) Osmosis is a possibility and sometimes very deep in the event that communication is prioritized over their autonomy needs. Their interactions will be outstanding if their mutual respect is maintained and, most importantly leaving room for freedom to each other which is the foundation for the growth of the air signs.

The water significations (Cancer, Scorpio, Pisces) can bring a small amount of trouble for Gemini since they're not expressive, and much more abstract, and they hinder Gemini from knowing what we expect from Gemini. If a intense physical attraction connects them, Gemini will hardly be in a position to feel loved in the way they would like to. Likewise, water signs could be overwhelmed by Gemini's apex of emotions.

Earth signs (Taurus, Virgo, Capricorn), Gemini is far too eloquent and their desire to be free is an ongoing worry for earth signs, who are extremely sassy. Gemini is a very solitary sign. Gemini can become a bit tense when it is feeling too much hold, but it will eventually disappear without having to look back. The relationship may work, but only with lots of compromise and trust on both sides which can be very challenging for both …

(Cancer (From the 21st of June through July 22)

The love compatibility Virgo, Cancer

What do you love what you like about Cancer The gentleness of his character and compassion and values-based beliefs and his family and his constant need to be stable.

What makes it work: Even though you're not within the same world, you may locate some waiting points to help your relationship flourish however it will not be simple.

What is the reason it doesn't work? If both of you are tied to your values and habits You don't share the same perspective on life and that could damage your relationship. Therefore, you'll need to develop a way of communicating and most importantly, to work through the differences between you.

Sex-Erotic Compatibility: You'll likely be extremely frustrated like the other and there is a very low likelihood that you'll be able to be able to agree.

The Cancer is among the most sensitive indications of Zodiac which is why it's a sign of caresses. an affinity, however it is also romantic with you. However it's an indication that may take some time to reveal its true nature to you, since it requires confidence and also to get to know his companion to as little as possible.

Even if he doesn't reveal it, Cancer prefers to be the one who is dominated, rather than being dominant. The trick is to do this with great care and gentleness. If you succeed, you'll likely get his blessing to test everything. Whatever you think is best.

Last but not least, remember that Cancer requires to be aware that emotions are shared. If he does not Cancer will be a bit numb and offer only just mediocre performances, at the very least ...

Signs that indicate Cancer is the most compatible erotic relationship: Cancer man: Cancer, Libra, Capricorn, Aquarius, Pisces Cancer woman: Cancer, Virgo, Libra, Aquarius

How can you seduce a Cancer?

A astrological sign could help you to understand the person's personality to help you attract her. Learn about what Cancer sign may be hiding, and how he prefers to be charmed and approached and Cancer is not able to keep you from attracting him!

The Cancer (From June 21 until July 22)

The Cancer requires reassurance and to be reassured that we are loved the Cancer for who it is. it is sure to be open to nice words and also to people who are affixed to the family values. You can charm him with the manner of gentleness, as this is a sign of someone who is not a fan of rapidity and is more attracted to appreciation and praise to be given to him.

Be aware of how to protect yourself and let him know that you care regarding his wellbeing and concerns, then there'll be no reason to stop him from sharing his thoughts and feelings with you.

Cancer Your astral love compatibility

Cancer Astrology will help to understand the other astrological signs , and help you determine which ones you are in sync with, and who you're most likely to enjoy your relationship. Are you ready to learn which zodiac sign is the best one for you?

The Cancer (From June 21 through July 22)

The Earth Signs (Taurus, Virgo, Capricorn) are great allies in meeting the emotional requirements of Cancer. If earth signs behave in a manner of prudence and sensitivity and sensitivity, they can be sure that Cancer to show them all the love they can. Their growth will be natural and two projects could provide the motivation for personal development.

In the case of these water significators (Cancer, Scorpio and Pisces) the partnership is best when the conversation is sincere, as Cancerians are averse to being misled and disillusioned Good communication is usually the main ingredient in an effective relationship. When it comes to the water signs, understanding is mutual. For the relationship to flourish, Cancer should not feel dominant, but rather, balanced.

The Fire indications (Aries, Leo and Sagittarius) Cancer is in constant doubt about its relationship to the sun to the sun. It is not comforted by the fiery actions that the signs of fire exhibit. Cancer is a shrewd and discerning person. Cancer must be questioned to show how much we love the Cancer, but he doesn't have a passion for anyone, but within the limits of reason. The opposite of this is the indications of fire!

The air signs remain (Gemini, Libra, Aquarius) and With whom your relationship is likely to be energetic! These signs are obsessed with independence, whereas Cancer is usually awed with its cocoon. The couple in this case will struggle with being in harmony because their individual needs will be unbalanced when they are together. If they truly are in love with each other. they'll need to find the perfect rhythm.

(Lion (From June 23 through August 22)

Compatibility in love Virgo, Leo

What do you like what you like about Leo his charisma, his sense connecting, his method of progressing through life, his charisma and determination.

What makes it work? You'll be able to manage the other. Therefore you'll be able to manage the Leo will always push you to be better than yourself, and you'll know how to think about it, be able to manage it and manage it.

What can make it impossible to be effective? Being very quiet, you might be unable to maintain the egocentricity of Leo who has to return everything to him. If you are in the opposite direction and being in your denial of yourself and your partner, you will have a difficult time having a long-lasting relationship.

Sex-erotic compatibility is a different story altogether. all. Here it is mostly a story about emotions.

The Leo loves to have someone make by his love, and especially when it's executed correctly! If he sees a powerful companion in you, he'll be completely free, especially when he senses a intense physical attraction to you.

He will be attracted by stunning places and attractive people, particularly those who are adept in making him want to be lusty!

Everything is important to Leo from the very first moment to the final each detail is crucial and influence the behavior of your friend So you've got the right cards to put this Lion prey to your will.

Signs that indicate Leo is the most harmonious erotic connection: Leo man : Gemini, Leo, Libra, Pisces

Leo woman Gemini, Leo, Virgo, Scorpio, Pisces

How do you seduce an Leo?

A astrological sign could help you to understand the person in order to attract her. Learn about the Leo sign is hiding, what they like to be approached and seduced. Leo is not able to keep you from attracting him!

Lion (From the 23rd of July through August 22)

The Lion 's aren't really spectators, but actors. They admire you and convince them into believing that they are so cherished at their real worth. But, you'll need to be a strong person as well as someone who is different from the norm. A flattery with him is the most effective way to reach your goals, but it must be done with care, since Leo is not naive.

If you pay him the attention he demands If you give him all the attention he needs, he'll be proud of you. But keep in mind that in all likelihood you will be the one who lets him be swept away by the connection.

Leo, your astral love compatibility

Leo Astrology can assist you know other signs of astrology and, consequently, let you know which signs you're most compatible and with whom you're most likely to find your love affair
flourish. Leo Are you eager to learn which zodiac sign is best for you?

Lion (From the 23rd of July until August 22)

Fire signs (Aries, Leo and Sagittarius) generally extremely in sync with Leo because they are extremely energetic and powerful. The desire for innovation is one of the main reasons they are all a part of, along with the desire to work on projects and constantly seek both sensual and intellectual satisfaction.

Air signs (Gemini and Aquarius) Libra as well as Aquarius), Leo can as well be hoping for a lovely relationship that is most importantly based on originality and fun. Leo is a lover of surprises by Love and what better than the signs of the air to give him a connection that is always in motion and filled with twists and twists. The Lion is always ready to respond in the event that we allow him breathe!

The Leo does not want to settle for the best, he is looking for the very best! This little lapse of pride can cause a rift with planets (Taurus, Virgo and Capricorn) since they tend to be reserved and don't appreciate the excitement very much. To be able to have a successful relationship both of them must convey to each other what's lackingand be able to maintain their relationship in harmony.

The Water indications (Cancer, Scorpio and Pisces) the Leo is at risk of becoming bored, being confined to a straitjacket that is too tense for his taste. The water signs can be somewhat too preoccupied in the Leo who wants a romantic relationship that is constantly in good working order. The relationship could last when one of them decides to let go of their desires towards the other, but the balance won't be equal.

(Balance (From to September 23, until the 23rd of October)

The love compatibility Virgo, Libra

What do you like what you like about Libra Your favorite qualities are: His sensuality, his appreciation for artistic finesse, his ability to communicate, his wit, communication, his desire to equilibrium.

What makes it be successful? You can create an unshakeable universe that is enriching and in a state of harmony as you are couples are both seeking peace and happiness. Your couple will walk with grace.

What is the reason it won't work? You may be unable to comprehend the decisions that are made by Libra who, while willing to make a commitment, will struggle to take the plunge and this sign won't be living up to your demanding and critical side.

Sex-Erotic Compatibility: Even if the beginnings of your relationship are pleasant as time passes, your relationship and seduction will eventually wear off!

The balance is likely to be one of the toughest to settle because it reflects his infamous indecisiveness and intense desire to experiment with doing it can feel a bit snubbed or not loved. Therefore, you will have lots of work to complete to impress her, however, when you play the love card carefully and are patient it will be possible to awaken her sexuality and shine!

The balance isn't she a huge fan of brief relationships. She prefers an overall sweet married life that allows him to expand his sexuality and be confident.

She is willing to be able to accept dominating and being controlled by others, but it's your responsibility to adjust to her speed!

Signs that indicate Libra is the most erotic compatibilityare: Libra male : Aries, Gemini, Cancer , Virgo, Libra,

Sagittarius Libra woman: Aries, Taurus, Cancer, Leo, Libra, Sagittarius

How can you charm an Libra?

The astrological signs can aid in understanding the person in order to attract her. Learn about the Libra sign is hiding, and its way of wanting to be wooed and embraced and this Libra isn't going to be able keep you from attracting!

Balance (From September 23 through the 23rd of October)

The balance of your life is unpredictable, so you must be patient and persuasive to reach your objectives. The Libra like people who are playful and energetic, yet solid, so don't appear too pushy or nimble at the risk of letting it slip disappearing fast.

It is important to be patient prior to giving all she has as she must be confident. So, expect to spend lots of time speaking with her and having to explain your intentions and feelings.

Scorpio, your astral love compatibility

The Scorpion, Astrology could help to understand other astrological signs, and help you determine the signs that you are most in sync with, and who you're most likely find your partner. Scorpio Are you prepared to discover which other zodiac sign will work for you?

Scorpio (October 24 until November 22)

With similar water signs to his (Cancer, Scorpio and Pisces), Scorpio manages to maintain a healthy balance as their needs are similar. Both physically and intellectually, Scorpio can flourish, and if they are that they are in a relationship that is healthy, Scorpio will give all their affection and affection.

Earth signs (Taurus, Virgo and Capricorn) are an excellent combination so long as Scorpio isn't influenced by the strength in the sign of earth. If the relationship is diplomatic and has a good communication between the two parties the relationship is likely to be mutually beneficial. However If the two parties adhere to their own beliefs, the relationship may quickly turn bitter and anger!

It is likely that fun will be the buzzword for these air sign indications (Gemini, Libra and Aquarius) However, it's only going to last some time. Unsatisfaction with the status quo will prevail on the Scorpio who can never be assured by the sign of air that is too busy to be in the present moment. In order for this relationship to be successful it is essential that both parties put their cards on the table and become unstoppable, but is that feasible?

The signs of fire (Aries, Leo and Sagittarius) are too superficial for a Scorpio seeking love and security. The initial passion will be merely a façade and if expectations are not fulfilled, Scorpio will fail to give new life to their relationship. Communicating will prove to be a huge issue, and their incessant competition can cause them to fall apart.

Libra Love your astral self compatibility

Libra Astrology can help you to understand the other astrological signs , and help you determine which ones you are most compatible and with which signs you are most likely to find your relationship blossom. Libra Are you prepared to discover which zodiac sign is the best one for you? Affirmation (From September 23 through October 23)

The signs of the air (Gemini, Libra, Aquarius) are her preferred ones as she is awed in their joy and desire to be constantly active. The Libra loves a good love, a solid and fulfilling love. She doesn't feel overwhelmed by the air signs and is able to give its strength and joy to the relationship.

In the fire signs (Aries, Leo and Sagittarius) she is able to discover captivating and passionate connections, but over time the relationship could become exhausting due to the fact that Libra is also seeking stability and harmony in her relationships. When the signs of fire are able to protect her and her partner, she'll be able to give up without a trace and let her entire person.

The signs of the earth (Taurus, Virgo and Capricorn) are a bit too prescriptive for her! The balance is a bit erratic by nature. She's having a hard time making decisions and earth signs are completely in control. The situation could turn into a drama, and for those Libra who is averse to conflicts, it can be extremely difficult to live!

There is no easy way to go when you are a water sign (Cancer, Scorpio and Pisces) since the apparent calm of the third actually conceals the deep sense of fear that Libra can't soothe.

The balance won't be there as the water signs aren't present in the moment, but they are in continuous motion. Their expectations are not the same to provide something that is meaningful over the course of the course of time.

(Scorpio(October 24 until November 22)

Compatibility in love Virgo, Scorpio

What do you like about Scorpio The sex attraction of Scorpio Their mysterious and mysterious mind, their desire to know, to comprehend.

What is it that makes it work? You were designed to be a team There is no doubt about that. One is able to please one another and the other being able to lead him to uncharted places. Your relationship will never be devoid of chilies or twists.

What is the reason it can't work? The frequent crisis of the Scorpio as well as its aggressive even cynical and even cruel side which you'll be in a position to defend yourself with your acerbic and critical spirit. You must learn to be respectful of yourself if you wish to succeed.

Sexual erotic compatibility: Astrology would like you to have a harmonious relationship and this isn't a bad thing because Scorpio is able to make you feel the most sensual aspects of you!

The Scorpio is an excellent strategist, as he'll let himself be seduced in order to gain more control over you in the future. Beware of their apparent lack of confidence or apathy, Scorpio is a sign that will eventually prefer to dominate you.

Expect to surrender to him because the more submissive you are, the more pleasure he gets, it will multiply, giving you with unforgettable moments.

To reach your goals by the help of a Scorpio You will have to establish a pattern where you gradually accept him as a partner, so the pleasure will last and last for a long the course of time, creating a long-lasting friendship between you.

Signs for which Scorpio is the most compatible erotic relationship: Scorpio man: Taurus, Leo, Virgo, Scorpio, Aquarius Scorpio woman: Scorpio, Aquarius

How do you seduce the attention of a Scorpio?

A astrological sign could help you to understand the person in order to attract her. Learn more about what the Scorpio sign has to offer, and also what he prefers to be attracted and enthralled, and this Scorpio is not able to keep you from attracting him!

Scorpio (October 24 until November 22)

To entice the attention of a Scorpio You will need show them that you are a person with something they don't! The entire process will revolve around the realm of persuasion and seduction. You should show your strengths, and you must not rely with your potential resemblance to another person, instead, focus on your complementary qualities.

The Scorpio is a patient Scorpio and can require you to wait for an extended time before he's willing to listen to your demands, but you must know that once you've convinced him that he will be a pleasant companion.

Chapter 8: Scorpio, your astral love compatibility

It is a sign of Scorpio. Astrology could help to understand other signs of astrology and let you know the signs that you are most at ease with and with who you're most likely be in love with. Scorpio Are you willing to learn which zodiac sign will work for you?

Scorpio (October 24 through November 22)

With similar water signs to Scorpio (Cancer, Scorpio and Pisces), Scorpio manages to achieve a balance since their desires are comparable. Physically as well as intellectually, Scorpio can flourish, and if they are that they are in a relationship that is healthy, Scorpio will give all their attention and sensuality.

The signs of the earth (Taurus, Virgo and Capricorn) can be a great combination insofar as Scorpio does not have to be subject to the strength that is associated with the Earth sign. If the relationship is diplomatic and has a good communication between the two parties understanding, it can be extremely beneficial. However If the two parties adhere to their opinions, the relationship could quickly become bitter and angry!

The word "fun" will be the guiding principle for those with air indications (Gemini, Libra and Aquarius) However, it's only going to last an extended period of time. Discontent will prevail against the Scorpio who cannot be soothed by an air sign. busy enough to enjoy the present. In order for this relationship to be successful the two parties must be able to play their cards straight in the game and be impervious, but is this feasible?

The signs of fire (Aries, Leo and Sagittarius) are too shallow for the Scorpio looking for love security. The love that is evident at first is just a gimmick and if expectations aren't met, Scorpio will fail to give new life to their relationship. Communicating will prove to be a huge issue and their relentless competition can lead to their demise.

(Sagittarius (From Nov. 23 until December 22)

The compatibility between love and romance Virgo, Sagittarius What you love about Sagittarius The generosity of his heart and soul and his desire to move, make a change from the routine, which means that everything you don't know about!

What is it that makes it work? You are able to get along very well and the Sagittarius sign helps your life more interesting and you view it in a positive manner. If you're up in the air, you'll be able to get it under control and become more realistic.

That means that it will not be successful: You'll be unable to fulfill the desire to experience the adventures of this sign that reveals fire to keep striving to achieve an ideal like it would have trouble staying in the right direction by your partner! Accept the differences of everyone!

Sexually-erotic compatibility: The Fire sign is not devoid of ways to ignite the powder, however you have to remain at ease!

The Sagittarius isn't easy, but he can get swept away by the circumstance and will offer the best of what you can If you truly have a good. He's someone who loves foreplay. The more satisfied he is with this issue and more, the more it will bring out his sexuality.

Also, When the Sagittarius loves someone, he will give uncounted amounts of attention to his lover and is keen to create an intimate and beautiful bond. but when he's not feeling inspired, he could simply become an uninspiring belt. for a long period of time without blinking an eye.

The Sagittarius is also a fan of good news, but he does not like to be domineering as he does not want to be dominated.

Signs that indicate Sagittarius has the highest compatible eroic aspects: Sagittarius man: Gemini, Libra, Sagittarius, Pisces Sagittarius woman: Taurus, Gemini, Libra, Sagittarius, Pisces

How can you charm Sagittarius?

The astrological signs can help you to understand the person better to lure her. Learn about what Sagittarius sign might be hiding and how they prefer to be wooed and embraced and this Sagittarius will be unable to be averse to you!

Sagittarius (From Nov. 23 until December 22)

The Sagittarius requires someone to help him achieve the thing they've always wanted to, so have things around your house that can entice and spark the interest of his. Be creative put your money on romance and you'll be able to touch it inside the soul!

However, be aware that Sagittarius is not a fan of disappointment, and if they discover that you've lied to him, he'll likely turn away from you with no regrets, but it's recommended to play your cards at the table from the beginning with him.

Sagittarius, your astral love compatibility

Sagittarius, Astrology can help you to know other signs of astrology and allow you to determine which signs you are most comfortable with and with which signs you are most likely to find your relationship work. Sagittarius Are you eager to discover which other zodiac sign is best for you?

Sagittarius (From the 23rd of November through December 22)

The Sagittarius can be found in different significations of fire (Aries, Leo and Sagittarius) but their expectations differ slightly. It is believed that the Sagittarius tends to be more love and gives lots of energy and a sense of humour if it gets a feeling of a tickle and can make him happy! The fire signs are able to live their passions in the present and are willing to give everything as long as they're constantly engaged.

The air indications (Gemini, Libra and Aquarius) and the Sagittarius will display an unending ability to express himself since he feels heard by the expressive air signs. However the Sagittarius must be the one who is in control to to show his total confidence. This isn't an easy task with air signs that are liberated and independent, however the Sagittarius is able to do this with a sense of discretion. !

The signs of the water (Cancer, Scorpio and Pisces) have a dual-edged attraction especially for Sagittarius who is attracted to them through their love for each other however, they are a distance due to their lack of expression. Long-term the relationship could prove to be very challenging especially for the Sagittarius who is never done needing to prove his love, and expect proofs of love that will be difficult to come by.

The planets (Taurus, Virgo and Capricorn) are too far-sighted for Sagittarius who requires a bit of a jolt for a sense of vitality. The key word for this type of relationship will be negotiation. They will need to let go of a lot of their beliefs in order to ensure that the relationship will last in the long run, but Sagittarius cannot stand being continually confined and not getting satisfaction.

(Capricorn (From the 23rd of December until January 19)

Compatibility in love Virgo, Capricorn

What do you find appealing about Capricorn? His need to be stable and maintain his focus, his confidence, and his sense of accountability.

What is the reason it works: You're a great couple and have lots in common. This means you'll be an enduring couple that can change over time as they go through difficulties!

What causes it to not work? Your main issue is the inability to communicate and the necessity to keep certain routines. In time, your life will turn into an ongoing routine. You must try to break out of this rut!

Sex-erotic compatibility: You've got similar expectations and for that , your relationship will endure!

The Capricorn is usually in agreement with himself about his sexuality. There isn't much to expect from him instead, he is a growing sexuality based on a lovely connection.

The Capricorn is able to think outside of the box, it's only on the condition that you take things to your own accord without realizing. It's a difficult game however, it can pay dividends, particularly if you are one to mix things up!

The Capricorn is a sign of the security and love However, don't be expecting a wild ride of love and excitement. Stability will still be the rule.

Signs that indicate Capricorn is the most of an erotic connection: Capricorn man: Virgo, Capricorn, Pisces

Capricorn female: Cancer, Virgo, Capricorn

How do you seduce the attention of a Capricorn?

The astrological signs can help you to understand the person in order to attract her. Learn about the Capricorn sign is hiding and what he enjoys being taken in and be charmed, and this Capricorn will be unable to keep you from attracting him!

Capricorn (From November 23 until January 19)

The Capricorn isn't an amazing individual, he is a lover of simplicity, and in particular tranquility. Therefore, there is no need to impress the Capricorn with outrageous behaviors and excesses of any kind. He won't be amazed, in fact. Instead, focus on logical words, a calm personality and outings with the culture to reach your objectives.

You can be sure that the Capricorn is also able to add a bit of crazy into his daily life, but he'll not reveal it until he is 100 100% certain of your intentions, so please be cautious!

Capricorn, your astral love compatibility

Capricorn, Astrology can help you to know other signs of astrology and, consequently, let you know which zodiac signs you're most compatible with , and with which signs you are most likely to find your love affair flourish. Capricorn Are you willing to discover which other zodiac sign is the best one for you?

Capricorn (From the 23rd of December through January 19)

Earth signs (Taurus, Virgo and Capricorn) share a lot of affinities, although there are few differences between the three. If the Capricorn is not feeling valued, he will become depressed and the relationship he has with his partner causes lots of worries. In general, the similar beliefs of Earth signs give an assurance and clarity that Capricorns are particularly fond of.

Water signs (Cancer, Scorpio and Pisces) ensure Capricorn gentleness and equilibrium In return it provides them with confidence and emotional stability. Their compatibility can lead to positive relationships when communicating is conducted in a clear manner and difficulties are dealt with in a diplomatic manner. The Capricorn feels content and relaxed by the well-balanced nature of water indications.

The Air signs (Gemini, Libra, Aquarius) The relationship between them is difficult to settle since the expectations are opposite. The Capricorn that seeks peace of mind won't be comforted by the unpredictable personality of air signs neither will they be entangled trapped in their desire for the freedom and social interaction. It is normal to make compromises so that everyone can find noon on their doorstep.

The signs of fire (Aries, Leo and Sagittarius) are a bit too enthusiastic for Capricorn who enjoys serenity and gentleness. The passion can last for a long time and fill Capricorn but the relationship is doomed when both parties fail to modify their approach to the long-term relationships.

(Aquarius (From Jan 20 until February 18)

Compatibility of love Virgo, Aquarius

What do you love you most about Aquarius What do you like about Aquarius? His human traits as well as his flair for innovation and curiosity, his desire for new ideas and new ideas.

What makes it be effective? You'll be able to communicate ideas, patterns of thinking, it's one of the strengths of your partnership that allows you to keep a the least amount of exchanges per key.

What is the reason it doesn't work? You won't always be at ease with an

Aquarius since you won't share the same points of attraction and your interactions will be done via touching or in a loopy manner, which is not the best way to go about looking at the long-term.

Sex-erotic compatibility: If you're in the love-friendship model it is not possible to find fulfillment, it's an affair to be viewed as a moment of tenderness , and not for anything else!

The Aquarius is similar to moods. They change! This makes it difficult to master him, however, you must be able to avoid becoming bored by the
Aquarius. Sometimes soft as a lamb sometimes wild as the lion, you'll never know the best way to go!

Attracted by fun and excitement, Aquarius will certainly know how to pull you into situations straight from his creative mind, and Aquarius will be able to inspire you and take lessons from you!

Be aware that Aquarius views everything as fun, but if you're too conventional or abrasive, they will not be able to keep you in the dark for long!

Signs for which Aquarius is the most compatible erotic relationship: Aquarius man: Cancer, Virgo, Scorpio, Aquarius

Aquarius woman: Cancer, Scorpio, Aquarius

How do you seduce an Aquarius?

The astrological signs can help you to understand the person better to lure her. Learn about the Aquarius sign reveals as well as the ways it wants to be wooed and embraced and how this Aquarius won't resist you!

Aquarius (From Jan 20 through February 18)

If you're looking to charm the Aquarius You will definitely be required to think outside the box and place your bets on the uniqueness and non-conformity. The Aquarius is an individualist He will be drawn to dreams, freedom-loving, and independent individuals, though he generally likes the majority of people.

But do not try to control it or alter it in any way, since Aquarius is always self-assured and, should you fail to adjust to his character It is best not to keep trying for seduction ...

Aquarius, your astral love compatibility

Aquarius, Astrology can help you know other signs of astrology and allow you to determine which signs you are most comfortable with and with which signs you are most likely to get your relationship flourish. Aquarius Are you eager to learn which zodiac sign the right one for you?

Aquarius (From Jan 20 until February 18)

The signs of the air (Gemini, Libra and Aquarius) offer a chance of a harmonious relationship for Aquarius who wants to have an active and harmonious exchange. The relationship between the couple is sweet, but infused with a touch of sexiness, which is essential to enhance the couple. If the boundaries of freedom are respect this relationship will be healthy and long-lasting.

The earth sign (Taurus, Virgo, Capricorn) The combination is challenging, but it's possible, if the Aquarius can move freely about. If doubts are raised, it's important to build the relationship on an unambiguous communication. If not both will remain locked in his own corner, trying to convince the other one to move forward. It could go on for a long time ...

Signs of Fire (Aries, Leo and Sagittarius) are able to are able to take Aquarius to nations they would never have attempted to traverse on their own, but after the joy of the moment the reality of returning is usually brutal for passionate Aquarius. stability. It is nevertheless possible and highly promising if Aquarius will allow himself to be ruled by the fiery personality associated with the signs of fire.

The relationships to the signs of water (Cancer, Scorpio and Pisces) are too dull for Aquarius to be able to achieve real satisfaction. Aquarius is a mutable sign. Aquarius will be moving ahead, and it won't take a step back and create its way through the short- and long-term plans. The water signs are rooted in the past. They use nostalgia as their motivation to continue to move forward which Aquarius is likely to be unable to accept, and will cause an enormous distance between them.

(Pisces (From Feb 19 through March 20)

The love compatibility Virgo, Pisces

What do you love you most about Pisces Its deep skin sensitiveness, its sensuality romanticism, its gentleness and altruistic nature.

What is it that makes it work? You attract yourself while you turn away from yourself. However, Pisces is a master of art and manner of cheering you up. And, very delicately, he is able to lead you into an enjoyable relationship.

What causes it to not be successful? Your contradictions the insanity of Pisces as well as its inaccuracy and, conversely, your savage side over-simple, maniacal too excessive!

Sex-erotic compatibility: If this feeling goes away, you'll not be disappointed. However, be aware because we could even say it's an indication that you be in the skin!

The Fish will accept all things, as long as we ask! Don't believe that he will not take initiative in your love. He is not going to do anything. On contrary He will be able to fulfill your most cherished desires will be done with pleasure.

He is more prone to a gentle and sexy manner rather than lovemaking infused by passion or even a bit of bestial, and this could keep him from finding enjoyment in it.

He's sometimes inactive that, even if his sexual life didn't suit him He would not do anything to alter the situation
... Some people like flexible partners who are like him, but others may struggle with his inability to take initiative.

Signs that Pisces has the highest compatibility with erotics: Pisces man: Aries, Taurus, Leo, Sagittarius, Pisces

Pisces woman: Taurus, Cancer, Leo, Virgo, Sagittarius, Capricorn, Pisces

How do you seduce an Pisces?

A astrological sign could aid in understanding the person's personality to help you attract her. Learn about the Pisces sign is hiding, how he prefers to be charmed and approached and this Pisces isn't going to be able keep you from attracting him!

Pisces (From the 19th of February through March 20)

The Fish is among the most beautiful zodiac signs but it's also the most difficult to catch! This means that you will have a lot of difficulties attracting it into your fishing nets. Some techniques will be needed to get your goals. Make him believe that he's the one to catch you up, despite walking around before him for the entire evening. In the end, stimulating the desire of his will be an effective strategy.

Be aware that a bit of force is not a bad thing as Pisces can be quite flexible but always make sure to go there smiling, it's the best strategy to attract him!

Pisces Your astral love compatibility

Pisces Astrology will help to understand the other astrological signs, and identify which signs you are most in sync with and , consequently, with whom you're most likely to find your love affair flourish. Are you eager to know which zodiac sign you are the best fit for you?

Pisces (From Feb 19 through March 20)

The zodiac signs that are water-based (Cancer, Scorpio, Pisces) clearly have plenty of appeal for Pisces eager to share emotions. They see love in a highly cerebral manner, and their peace is usually a gentle and a cosy relationships. The only thing is that Scorpio can discover Pisces slightly too romantic for their taste However, that shouldn't cause any problems!

The Earth signs (Taurus, Virgo and Capricorn), Pisces can form an equilibrating relationship only when the earth signs don't limit them by their power and control. The signs of Pisces are:

Numerous complementarities exist and the Pisces is willing to give up the reins of their partnership to the person he is with if they feel at ease and secure with a task that is just as important in his perception.

The signs of the air (Gemini, Libra and Aquarius) draw the Pisces however, some disillusions could ruin this wonderful meeting due to the fact that the Pisces requires direction to progress which the air signs aren't enough able to. They can't give the Pisces. It is therefore possible to arrange to ensure that Pisces is content in his everyday relationships.

The fire signs (Aries, Leo, and Sagittarius) aren't likely to be able to find the luxury they want in Pisces since Pisces can be a bit stoic to fit their needs. Their opposing nature is so that it can be compared to fire or ice, however at the end of the day it is the fire that always manages to beat the ice and, in the end, is just a thin small puddle in the water ...

The ideal vacation for you is Virgo in accordance with your Astrological sign

What's your dream holiday? Where should you travel this season? What is the ideal place in which to recharge? Do not let luck decide your fate. Our Astrologer Chris Semet, gives you all the information you need to know about the exact location and date for your next trip ...

The sign of the earth which is which is ruled by Mercury (practice modernity, practice) as well as Ceres (harvesting fields and agriculture). ...) lush landscapes trees that are green or fall colors vast expanses of meadows, fields, cottages rejuvenate you and lift your spirits.

The best places to go are areas with hills and in which the fauna and flora are abundant. You prefer temperate climates and you'll feel at home in an area where water and land mix forests and marshes as well as sand and sea.

In order to avoid the crowd You prefer peace and quiet places in which you can rest and relax. The key words you should be using are peace, harmony and pure ...

Holiday spots for Virgos:

Touraine, Mayenne, Aquitaine Basin, Charente, Vendee, Limousin, Flanders, Picardy, Belgium, Scotland, Ireland, Sweden, Austria, Canada, Polynesia, Marquesas Islands, Seychelles,

Reunion, Cape Verde Islands ..., Nepal, Bhutan, China, India.

You aren't a fan of the unknown and can't imagine daily life without comfort as well, which is why, as your companion, the Lion you are a fan of accommodations in hotels or apartments that are seasonal.

Unlucky couples with love compatibility is a subject that can be explored through astrology. With the help of celestial signs, we are able to understand how things work for couples and the flaws that may be able to fix based on the astrological sign of our birth and the sign for our companion.

Astrology is an excellent method to answer questions about love. It doesn't matter if it's relationship accounting, or anyone else on the lives of couples The stars could give you some clues.

The flaws in the couples' astrological significations

Find the small imperfections and mistakes that every astrological sign has. By identifying these flaws, you can work on your own performance and avoid falling into the same traps.

Aries is a professional who takes things to his own hand. In the case of a love story you cannot manage all things. Therefore, he must be able to allow things go. Let go is the most important word!

Taurus is a sign of stability and security. Taurus represents an astrological symbol of earth's element The Taurus loves the concretization and security. When it comes to love, Taurus tends to be a bit protective and jealous. There are flaws that he has to be careful not to choke the other.

Gemini are great at communicating however, they ... have difficulty understanding the root of the issue. Geminis aren't able to share the most important aspects of their thinking, which can cause difficulties in communication between couples. They must be honest to progress in a positive direction.

The astrological signification of Cancer is scared of suffering. Because he is too protective and avoiding letting people approach. He needs to learn to let loose to make the real bond with his companion. The Leo strives to always perform at the highest level. In the same way, he wants his partner to be at the top of their game as well. He has high standards. It is crucial to accept the flaws and flaws of each other.

The Virgo zodiac sign is very particular. He desires everything to be flawless ... and even his love life! Accepting that there will be some conflicts and miscommunications and disagreements, he can be able to see the bigger picture and appreciate the minor hiccups within his romantic story.

Libra is a lover of communication and meet new people and take part with new things. She isn't a great at finding a partner and settling. It is important to stop getting excited when she finds the person who truly suits her. It's not always greener where you are!

Find out more about how each astrological sign respond to the issues?

Scorpio has a tendency to be a dramatist ... What's a love affair without passion? He's not interested! But living in a tense relationship can be exhausting. The roller coaster ride for the duration of time is not long-lasting. It is crucial to realize that argument and love that is impossible don't work over the long run.

The Sagittarius Astrological sign is one that is a lover of fun and discover new things. Habits and routines are not enough to make him wish. He abandons his dream whenever his daily life gets too boring. He needs to become aware of the pleasures of life every day and put aside the pursuit filled with fun, which will cause him to be lonely.

Capricorn is known for putting their work life ahead of their personal lives. Capricorn should never forget his family and friends, as well as those who share his life as a result of this, otherwise they could end up becoming bored.

Aquarius frequently tests their partners to determine if they're truly in love. If they can open up and trust, he may enjoy pleasant surprises in his relationship.

Pisces can be confused. They're not able to make decisions, particularly in their private lives. If it's about deciding between two individuals, to remain or go to a different spouse, to be committed and to not ... They have to be able to make a decision and stick with it to achieve satisfaction.

Your sexuality based on your astrological sign not realize that your zodiac sign is significant influence on the way you feel about your libido. Do you have any questions about why you're engaging in bed or the reason you're an aristocrat in Kamasutra? This is the answer. You might be amazed. You can be surprised Naturally!

Aquarius: honesty is the most important thing

You're independent and confident. Therefore, when you fake an orgasm to save the ego of a man, does is not much is going to be a problem for you.

You're not sure the purpose. You'd rather show your companion how to make you look cum.

You can also become bored quickly. If your only night-time romance is a missionary, you leave.

What amazes your spouse the most is how fast you dress when the party is over.

The most unpleasant thing about sexual sex is the fact that it can cause you to develop the taste buds go numb, snuggling after sexual activity.

Pisces: You are in tune with your intuition.

One thing is certain that you're knowledgeable about sexual sex! You're sensitive, generous and sensitive, you are able to determine what it takes to bring your partner to the seventh heaven.

Be cautious, it's essential to give but it is equally important to receive. Do not be afraid to explain to your friend what is really getting you from the bottom.

What does your partner think? that he's lucky to have you as a partner.

The most unpleasant thing about sexual intimacy is when he's got an unintentional orgasm and then he sleeps in the first two minutes of sexual sex.

Aries: you're passionate. The ultimate goal is to be able to the level of orgasm. You're doing everything in your ability to achieve it.

Your partner is awestruck by your attitude and is always willing to try new ideas to help you achieve your goals.

What is it that attracts your partner the most is your talent as gymnast.

What do you dislike about sex? When your partner is taking too long to get an orgasm.

Taurus: you love doing things right and take your time . are patient and dedicated to every aspect of your life. Your loved ones appreciate your commitment and you feel very fortunate to have you as their partner.

What attracts your lover most? Your heavenly kisses?

The one thing you don't like about sexual sex is when you're in the mood for an orgasm , and suddenly your partner's position changes.

Gemini is the queen of Kamasutra

In the selection of sexual or partner roles there are plenty of options. The issue is, you usually struggle to make decisions. Don't get caught up in the details. Simply be you!

Since when you finally choose a partner and your loved ones are shocked by they're not sure. You're a great shot!

They are enthralled by how they communicate when you're looking to test something different.

What is the thing that entices your partner most? Your suggestions for sex-related role plays. One thing you dislike about sexis telling your partner that you're already planning to move your position after three minutes.

Gemini, also called the queen of Kamasutra!

Cancer: the emotional it is very difficult to enjoy sexual intimacy without feeling. A few one-night dates are good for you.

The best way to do this is to do it with at the other person in the eye. Even when you are doubtful about your own abilities.

You must know whether you're doing the right thing If you're the greatest shot he's had. It's rare to ask questions in public, but you want to be sure!

People are quick to get in love with the person you are. What could be more perfect? You're so charming and funny.

Your self-confidence isn't always a good thing. can be a trap for your self-confidence. Therefore, stop putting yourself in doubt constantly, there's no need to worry! What surprises your partner the most is the fact that you inform them about your ex when you've finished having sexual sex.

The one thing you don't like about sexual sex is having in the bathroom after having a sex. You'd rather enjoy this time with your beloved.

Leo You've got confidence in yourself.

You're asexual, you are a sex lover and you love being in love with someone. Your partner reciprocates it to you. He is a lover of be with you.

You're constantly 100%, and want to be acknowledged. Your self-confidence is an asset to having fun and getting it.

What does your partner think about you is that they think they are less than you in nearly every way.

The one thing you don't love about sexual sex is that you haven't put up a mirror on your ceiling to look at yourself when you're having sexual relations.

Virgo You don't trust you. If your partner does not say how amazing you've been, you can get angry fast.

In addition, you are a madman who asks him each time if he has an opinion following your legs are on the floor: "So did you like it? What did you think? ". It's just a matter of trying to become better.

Being shy by nature and prone to a slow time to consider the most important question. However, when you're being launched, you're not prevented from doing so.

What impresses your partner the most is your understanding of sexual sex. You're the best You are an expert on the erogenous zones, how to go about getting orgasmic ...

The one thing you don't love about sexis cleaning.

Virgo You must be assured!

Libra The sexting expert You love sending sexts. You're a pro at bringing tension. You and your partner have a fervent desire to show love to you in the aftermath of your long conversations.

What is it that your partner admires about you is your mastery of French language.

The most unpleasant thing about sexual sex is the need to be asked what you really need. What is the reason they can't just guess?

Scorpio The Scorpion: You're extremely intense. Everyone believes that you're amazing in your bed. Only your companions have the chance to discover what you really are worth.

You're sensual, without trying and foreplay is not a source of secrets for you.

Some people believe that you're not the kind of person to snuggle in the arms of your lover after a sex session But they're incorrect.

What you love about your partner you: the things you say by licking your lips.

The thing I don't like about sexual activity is that everyone believes you don't want to be around your former partners. Simply because you're a sexual professional doesn't mean that you don't feel emotions.

Sagittarius is the sign who makes everyone laugh. sexual relations in your presence is never a blast. You're full of fun and there is nothing ever uncomfortable with you.

You are among the rare people who can throw an insult right in the middle of the room without causing any disruption or annoyance to one of the others.

Your optimism and enthusiasm makes you very attractive. With you, other girls feel that they are the most attractive.

What is it that your partner admires about you is the fact that you're always ready for another round.

The thing that you hate about sexual sex is that you're so comfy sleeping that you struggle to get out of the bed with people you've had a sex with.

Capricorn is the most refined You are a fan of the most expensive silk sheets, sex toys and luxurious lingerie. It's true that you're an apprehension. Why wouldn't you?

The only drawback is that you will really are awed by your colleagues. Even if you're not doing it intentionally!

What they consider to be rude is actually sincerity. If you can find the perfect person the sparkles.

What is it that your spouse loves about you is your collection of lingerie. It's like you've never had mismatched underwear in your entire life.

The most unappreciated thing about sexual intimacy is sleeping in another's bed. You do not have your memory foam mattress or pillow that is hypoallergenic, and the satin sheet ...

10 indicators that you aren't sexually compatible. Having sex on the first date can be stressful. This is so much stress that the first experience is typically not the best. It's normal. For some couples, who are even in love, even in bed, mayonnaise doesn't have a place. It's nothing to be related to love or attachment or attachment, and it doesn't have anything to do with have anything to do with the performance of also. These couples aren't sexually in love. Here are 10 indicators that are never failing.

In love there are those who have found that precious equilibrium that is between physicality and psychic.

Then there are the sexual friends. They aren't keen on being with each other. However, their bond is a lusty pleasure for the body.

There are also their frontal counterparts that love each with one another and love their relationship, yet are not averse to any sexual excitement.

Here are 10 indicators that your relationship is in the latter category.

Rarely do you have sex in a hurry.

There's no way to seduce you. In the arms of one another or jumping onto him after he gets home, getting late due to an unexpected need... it is not a thing that happens to us.

There is no solution that can work for both simultaneously.

There's always someone who likes to be appreciated, but not simultaneously. Together, it's his turn.

You're used to being alone. Not only from time to the time. Every day. This isn't unwise, even if you're not able to have it all together, but to enjoy a bit of pleasure by yourself.

However, when it's the norm for your entire sexual life there's plenty to think about.

You are always staring at the sky.

Once it's done and the line is repeated repeatedly: "Oh no! You're done? It's a shame, because I was hoping to reach there". However, there was nothing to see. The odd stained carpet stain was an curiosity.

You've had a sexual encounter while watching the TV.

It is true that having sexual relations in the background of JT isn't sensual However, you mustn't talk about it because you fear your partner is actually watching TV while you are having a sex.

You do and, by the way, you too.

You show your love is due to the celebration of a birthday or holiday. In these situations you do it more for obligation and not simply out of love.

You're having a problem with your rhythm.

When one of you begins to get really into this, your partner will make an abrupt change in speed. Too quick or too slow, what ever it is, we all know that it destroys everything.

You don't want to be having sexual sex while having. Never. If one person is as hot like a blaze while the other is exhausted or busy, or uneasy ... It's all good. are great to make every excuse to not create a romantic relationship.

Your libidos do not match. You need six relationships per week, while the other requires only has two or three.

In terms of sex it is not a either a good or bad amount of relationships each week. In your case there's always someone who is irritated at not getting their needs met.

The frustration of the relationship isn't good.

If your friend's best friend claims that she's always having an orgasm, you won't trust her.

But achieving orgasm each time is feasible. Actually.

Astral chart: 18 surprising surprises that the stars may keep in reserve ...

It's great to have that the influences of stars as well as the temperaments associated with Pluto for Aquarius young ladies however, to truly complete my birth chart might be added to that listing ...

The Aquarius woman doesn't seem to be able to work well with Taurus. Taurus guy ... however, she's still in love with him.

Dreamy and sensitive Dreamy and sensitive, the Aquarius native Aquarius is gifted with artistic talents ... as well to avoid giving her any trouble she prefers to leave the Taurus man paint the walls by himself.

The number she has is 7. Her tree is pine, and her gemstone is sapphire ... however, she loves diamonds.

She's down to earth and does not believe in the power of divination ... even if she's spending her time on magic-voyance.com it's only to have amusement.

It is said that the Aquarius woman is extremely connected to her inner world ... And she leaps up to the ceiling whenever she sees that the Taurus man shaves the beard's hairs lying in the bathroom.

Fantastic romantic, she's obsessed with strong emotions ... And gets to the forefront of insanity by picking to be a person who is a fan who is a fan of "Mario Kart". The concordance between Mars and Pluto beneath the skies of Saturn provides an Aquarius woman a fiery temperament ... therefore, don't disturb her when you watch "Girls".

Infatuated with cocooning, she is committed to wellbeing ... therefore she must spend many hours under blankets enjoying chocolate. Professional, she loves to be part of a team ... so long as you follow her.

Active, she tries the Hula hoop, oriental dancing as well as rollerblading, watercolor, as well as plumbing ... so , no she did not have time to purchase the Pains Au Lait.

Aquarius represents air signs ... this is why she has missed swimming once more. A calm and discrete person by nature She is prone to falling asleep ... during evenings which make her feel uncomfortable.

In relationships in love, the Aquarius woman is not prone to marry ... and well after when she decides that the Taurus would like to take away his PEL to give her an expensive ring she would like to talk about the issue.

If you are an Aquarius woman believes she's right, nobody will be capable of changing her opinion ... which is very annoying to all the people who attempt to change their minds!

Her ingenuity and creativity is awe-inspiring. often irritates ... She's certainly not queen of Uno for nothing.

In a way, it is enchanting to people from Aries along with Sagittarius ... Taureans actually have a keen interest in being cautious.

The planet that controls the sign of her is Uranus ... And she isn't sure the location of it.

Anxious, unpredictable, and impulsive The Aquarius woman is severely deficient in moderation ... that just illustrates the birth chart of her should not be taken for granted.

The sexual profile of the astro for Taurus Gemini, the Taurus Gemini sex sign Taurus Gemini is a sex sign Taurus

Do you feel more passionate than Aries or gentle as Cancer? Find out your sexual profile.

A sign of the Earth that is ruled by Venus the planet of beauty and love, you're that is joyful and cerebral.

If you're an epicurean is a good chef, you are able to enjoy all the delights in life, even when you're not always able to be. You can't imagine your day-today life without love and you're also very exigent.

Don't be your partner that wants to. In a relationship, if you're in an intimate relationship, you establish numerous rituals to reassure you.

Love in Taurus requires the sensitivity and gentleness. Therefore, we say that you need to be groomed, and to do that, your partner will need to win.

Taste, touch and hearing are three senses that have to be stimulated in order to ascend to seventh heaven.

What's Taurus and sex?

If you enjoy a sluggish hug and hugs, you're looking forward to a pleasant experience. So, for him, the enjoyment will gradually be at its highest point and then fade away with fireworks.

Monsieur Taureau with his reserved or shy airs is an absolute center in the realm of "carnal" and consequently sensuality. The longer the duration the more enjoyable! He will never forget the preliminary steps that are his appetizer.

The dreams of Taurus. Taurus The Taurus fantasies are not particularly innovative or radical. Games that involve food and stimulate appetites are very popular. areas of erogenous in Taurus.

Chapter 9: What are the stones from the Virgo sign?

The primary stones of the Virgo sign are topaz and aventurine. They are the two mineral which best represent the sixth sign of the zodiac.

For the aventurine that is shown on the left is believed to be to have the capacity to remove negative energies from the surroundings that is associated with this zodiac sign. They also create a balance between the physical and spiritual.

Aventurine has qualities that promote happiness and guard against health problems particularly those that affect the mouth.

The topaz is, however is a gem which is able to enhance Virgo's intellect and intuition This is the reason it offers him the tools to help him protect himself by increasing these capabilities.

They are the primary stones that provide protection to Virgo However, there are many other stones which favor this sign. For instance, the most lucky stones for Virgo include rutile, topaz amber, amber, and amethyst. However, there are many more that can give you huge advantages. Be attentive to the sections below and begin familiar with the stones.

1 Amethyst

This stone offers Virgo the ability to maintain their mental as well as emotional stability and also the ability to remain neutral, to have mental clarity, and to be more humble. This helps those that are born with this sign will gain more strength to not be frustrated when circumstances don't happen as expected and help them succeed in the future by having focus and a sense of objectivity when working on it.

22. Amber

The amber stone can benefit people that are born in this sign, by increasing their awareness and clarity, enhancing their creativityand enabling to open their minds. It is therefore advisable to have her on hand whenever you require thoughts and ideas and also when you want to attempt to think more openly and let go of closed-minded thoughts.

3-Sodalite

We also suggest Virgo to purchase sodalite stones and keep it in their vicinity whenever they wish to unwind and more positive and enthused, get rid of their prejudices and rekindle their passion. This allows people to be more relaxed and allows them to do whatever they would like to do, without stressing too much, and being present in the moment.

4-Fluorite

Fluorite is an ideal stone to Virgo who must work with spontaneity and intelligence because it helps both of these elements work well for these individuals. This means that the ability to be resourceful and impulsive that Virgos are able to possess can be increased.

5-Rutile

The stone is less well-known than the others, but it is a great stone for the Virgo. Most importantly, it assists you to overcome fears and problems even those that might be hidden. Rutile is a gemstone that helps Virgo become stronger and push them to reach their limitations, step outside of the comfort zones and as a result, conquer their fears.

6-Pink quartz

In conclusion the rose quartz stone that is not to be missed in the life of Virgo. It is also one of the most beneficial gemstones for Taurus.

The primary impact of this mineral on those who take it is to help people let go of buried emotions and emotions. This helps them over come problems of all kinds particularly in the realm of love which is an extremely effective tool to prevent breakups and feel more confident about oneself and, consequently, improve self-esteem and feel a sense of love for someone.

Virgo Lucky Numbers

If there's something which can aid us in improving the chances we get in life, it is numerology. Knowing the significance of numbers can bring us to the highest success and, if we don't know them, could lead to the greatest loss. This is why it is important to consider the primary and secondary numbers which are the most significant for Virgo as they don't have the primary lucky number, which is an indication of their complicated nature.

Numerology: The most lucky numbers of Virgos are 10, 15, and 27.

The number 10 is the symbol of peace and unity. The fact that it is the number 10 and the number 0 indicates that this is an introvert with a great desire to think and all that is related to the intellect is taking place. This is why it is the number should be taken into consideration when it comes to working. Furthermore, it's compatible with numbers 2 and 5.

However the number 15 is a number which indicates positive intentions, luck and a person who is hardworking. In this scenario both numbers suggests that the person who is successful in his life, however, for that, it will be important for him to keep challenging himself. In this regard the number 15 is a perfect match for love. Everything connected to love, when we join it on the 15th regardless of the way we do it, it'll be an absolute success.

The number 27 is an ideal number to represent money. Everything we do that involves to the world of finances and numbers will be a success for us. However, the number asserts that it is a certain type of care on behalf of Virgo however, not everything should be believed in this particular number. It is important to consider the combinations that can be constructed with other numbers. Combinations that include the numbers 8 and 6 are the most beneficial.

Combining these numbers means that we are closer to luck, however it is important to consider other aspects such as numbers that aren't favorable for us or other indicators that indicate we could be more efficient at work or love. To define luck, we should take our cues from the basic number, which is on the number 3. It is the numerology for love and luck as well as of peace and intelligence that is in perfect harmony to 1. People with high motivation and creativeness.

Chapter 10: What's the color Virgo's most adored?

In the sign of Virgo We can observe Mercury as the planet. Mercury as the principal leader, the planet is typically associated with the reds with the most dark shades and it is the reason that browns are subject to the rule of this zodiac sign.

Other colors that are connected to this sign of Virgo include Beige which is similar to mustard and is linked to yellow, which is an additional color which plays a significant part in the home of the zodiac. The multicolored color is another color that is attached to the zodiac sign.

In the synthesis, we can observe from the color choices already mentioned in the previous paragraph that Virgo is a summation of the other signs in terms of color, we then can see the different colors within the rule for this particular sign.

The color brown is a symbol of responsibility at its most profound sense, and is associated with deep science and great innovations towards the experimental realm. If the brown color is visible, we will see a wise person however, it does not convey the same wisdom as we have seen in other signs using the gray color. Gray is more connected to the conceptual plane, brown in the trunks of trees symbolizes practical experience. Those people with this color be the ones who have experienced the most extreme things.

The most well-known brown color is one that is stable for a long time and is closely linked to masculine activities, and it's the color associated with these traits found in males. When brown turns a darker red hue, it can be seen as clearly the meaning behind the conclusion of a time and a clear symbolism can be observed in the autumn of leaves and is visible in harvest, it's the color of the beginning of learning, and also the conclusion of a cycle and the beginning of a new cycle.

We've seen a variety of ways to interpret the color yellow. In its synthesis, it is possible to claim that it is an opulent color and the more intense it, the more chance of obtaining stability and strength The lighter it is, the higher opportunities of finding negative aspects which is why it is advised to choose bright yellow colors that are intense.

The most lucrative professions for the Virgo

The Virgo people aren't suitable for jobs where the chaos of daily life and shifting priorities are the norm. They are more attracted to a career which allows them to exercise full control of their work and environment. Virgo generally has an excellent reputation for their excellent quality and an unblemished track record.

Virgo requires the ability to set clear expectations and direction. The sign can easily become stressed if the directions they receive are unclear or if there are any last-minute changes. The employee can be motivated perform within the established norms and adhere to the company's policies.

For Virgo the most rewarding careers include:

1- Tax auditor

Virgos are well-known throughout the world for their keen sense of details, their critical nature, and a keen eye for numbers. They have a remarkable ability to handle financial concerns. The challenge of this will not win you an award in a popularity contest. But they can get enormous satisfaction from getting to the root of the issue and feeling more confident. The task of a Tax auditors is to spot fraud and errors.

2- Nutritionist

An intense desire to learn about nutrition and health could lead certain Virgos in this route as a career. One method to make this world more sustainable to help people learn to maintain their health through healthy nutrition practices. Virgos follow their own advice and are able to share their own experiences. But, Virgo may tend to advocate a diet that is too strict. There are many people who have an idealistic view of food.

33 Naturopath

The natural curiosity of Virgo about health and healing could be an enjoyable way to investigate. They're always trying new the use of vitamins, herbs and healthy food items; they may also opt to explore scientific research in depth. This is a lucrative option and could attract Virgo because of their need for security. Virgos always seek perfection in themselves and other people. They can also suggest changes to their lifestyle professionally and without others thinking they're control freaks.

4 Professional Household Cleaner

The home life of Virgo is a constant chaos of chores, laundry and constant lodging. Why not earn money to experience this clean and tidy look as a pro cleaning service? The perfectionist in Virgo can be extremely helpful when specific standards are needed. Virgo will complete the task in accordance with instructions, and then ensure that everything is polished and sparkling. There won't be any sign of dirt, fingerprints or grime that can be hidden from the eyes of the discerning Virgo.

5 Executive assistant

This sign is organized efficient, effective, and displays excellent attention to the smallest of details. This is a great trait for managing someone else's schedules and other things, especially when the person is extremely active or significant. Virgo adeptly manages functions and schedules meetings, schedules and even trips. He or she won't be unhappy that the boss delegates other tasks to him, for example, cleaning the home, shopping for personal items writing mail, or conducting various errands. Because this is really two jobs all in one managing your own schedule as well as your boss's schedule, Virgo assistants must be adept in multitasking.

6- Statesman

This is a fantastic career for those with an obsessed Virgo mind. Analyzing and collecting data for financial, business, or government industries could be a dream. Statistics and percentages collected in huge databases are tools of trade. Virgo would like to play a part in determining divorce rates or the odds to win the lottery.

7 Archivesist

Another job that grants Virgo the ability to classify and categorizing is the archivist. A lot of Virgos have plenty of experience in this field because as children, they made lists and compilations of comics and comics. The volumes are assigned, and the manuscripts are submitted to the digital scanner by the hands of Virgo. They don't join this industry to make financial gain, but because of the joy of ordering. However, having to work with dusty and old papers indicates allergy sufferers face a regular risk to a successful occupation.

8- System analyst

If there's a problem in the flow of information or system, Virgo is the person to contact. Virgo can fix and tidy up both databases as well as systems. There is no one other than Virgo in the Universe has the patience to locate and remove duplicate entries and obsolete information. With perseverance and determination, Virgo will step in and ensure that computer systems operate smoothly , and any technical issues will be gone.

9- Technical

In the field or in the laboratory, Virgo is the person who is determined to gather the details and data, keep track of the results and write reports. His renowned attention to detail and meticulousness to detail result in rock-solid results. They can make their colleagues insane with the amount of duration of the work or occasionally look over the information but the work is completed properly. Don't ask them to take care of their lunch items since they'll need to complete an outstanding spreadsheet and won't return until 3pm.

10- Welder

This occupation requires a high degree of skill, precision and a steady and steady hand. If you make a mistake, the structure may crack or the equipment may fail. Virgo is certain that every weld is of the best quality and is in line with industry standards. Since he doesn't want to be held accountable, he'll do all to ensure that the welding is perfect. Additionally, he'll get be dressed in suits as well as protective equipment, be paid handsomely for making lots of noise, and never be accused of a crime.

Compatible with the other signs

Aries and Virgo Aries and Virgo have a relationship, but they are not the same personalities

We have two distinct personality types because Virgo tends to perfection, and always looking for ways to be noticed for his mistakes, his critiques Aries can't take and so it is a type of continuous struggle between them to decide the right side.

Aries and Virgo are part of a cardsinal constellation, Aries is mutable and Virgo. In general, their hopes for their futures are generally positive, but it depends on the field to the field to which they are connected; which is to say that in the field of professional work they form a nearly perfect partnership.

If Aries and Virgo decide to complete work jointly, the results generally positive because they're both people who have known worth in their respective work activities, but also to each having the essential qualities that compliment one another. Each other's working hours.

If Aries is stressed and angry, Virgo will keep calm and begin to organize; because of this they are able to maintain keep their balance. In the realm of sentiment, the scenario is typically very distinct. The occurrence of disputes is commonplace. the real world, they fight over all sorts of things including feelings, money, jealousy, and endless list of.

It's more obvious that they are different personalities however, instead of fighting over it, they could recognize the strengths and weaknesses in their relationship, the things are going to be much better between Aries and Virgo will be much more harmonious and they'll create a fascinating, complicated together... The effort would be worth it! pain!

Taurus with Virgo and Virgo, a strong relationship as two couples

They are both Taurus along with Virgo both are Earth signs. their relationship is strong, as the aspects that affect the economy are recognized and, even though Virgo is known to criticize frequently and make continuous comments, Taurus does not remain unresponsive, it responds and establishes the bar which allows him to be a partner with mutual respect and understanding between the two characters.

Taurus is one of the fixed signs, as well as Virgo is one of those mutable significations however, although at first glance it appears that the fixed sign and changeability are not compatible however, they are not. In any event your ascendants and be a major factor for or against your union.

Their workplace relationships are generally not the best ones due, in particular due to their extreme caution which can cause them lose opportunities that come up. But, the majority of Taurus and Virgo individuals are highly productive and have the necessary skills that allow them to succeed in what they want to achieve in their field.

If they are a couple the expectations will be higher because in all likelihood they consider themselves soul-mates. This is precisely that reason they interact in a very passionate and natural manner.

The problem is that their timidity can hinder the formation of an actual relationship. However, if you can resolve that minor issue and your relationship develops, it will be able to progress slowly towards the things you desire to achieve: love. Taurus and Virgo are in love with one another that surpasses all other
love. Congratulations!

Gemini with Virgo A relationship that is that is full of criticism

While both signs have the identical ruler and planet Mercury is manifesting in a different way. Virgo seeks out the finer details and finds flaws in everything and it is a snub. The problem gets worse when Mercury retrogrades, because during these times there are constant arguments and even if you do not stop them from blaming you or your Virgo partner is not able to speak up whenever he is not happy about things, your relationship will become complex and weakens.

Gemini and Virgo are a couple in which the same quality is combined: both are mutable signs of the zodiacal wheel. In general, their unions are fluid and somewhat or not so compatible, depending on the region that their relationships take place.

Their relationships with their employers are generally more favorable than the relationships that they can get. If Gemini and Virgo are working side-by-side and cooperate, it's not uncommon to see them form amazing bonds of loyalty. They also do not be competing with one another In fact they typically cooperate in order to reach their objectives. This way If one area is devoted to a particular task, the remaining part will be devoted to another task while avoiding becoming in the way and hindering.

If they are a couple their romantic relationships become more difficult, but in turn, they're equally attractive and thrilling even though they have enough distinctions, which is precisely this reason, they are more likely to have close relationships.

The final thing that is crucial to the smooth functioning of their marriage is the constant communication that they have; Gemini and Virgo can be able to talk for hours about anything about the future and the past and how much they cherish one another, etc.

Cancer in conjunction with Virgo and Virgo, the connection of the affinity of ideas and empathy

They are both passionate about family and home, and even though Virgo has a personality that is extremely vulnerable to criticism constantly He is able to comprehend Cancer when he debunks his arguments due to his instincts. Virgo assists Cancer to get his feet back in the moments where fantasies seem more important than reality, and it is a great combination. Cancer's patience and understanding will make up for any mishaps.

Cancer is a sign that belongs to the so-called cardinal sign of the zodiac, and Virgo is one of the zodiac signs which are part of the mutable signs. So, generally speaking their relationships will be positive in all of the areas to which they interact as they share many traits. Their relationships with their employers are beneficial not just in terms of economics however, they also benefit in other ways.

Two hardworking people and in a group, more so. Similar to that, they typically like working together because they have the same criteria and methods of living. In addition, Cancer and Virgo attach importance to the world of the physical this is why they don't hesitate to keep striving to make it better.

If they are a couple then the likelihood of enjoying an exciting future together is extremely and they will support, respect and support one another all the time. The Cancer sign Cancer aids another sign in financial terms and Virgo can do the same thing with Cancer however, it is not materially.

The most negative aspect of their relationship is the tendency of Virgo to pursue independence without relying on any other side. In any event, Cancer and Virgo know how to live happily The rest will arrive mostly on their own.

Leo with Virgo A relationship that is characterized by tensions

There's nothing that can make you more than constant criticism. In that way, Virgo knows how to accomplish this because the Virgo is constantly looking for faults in everything because of his outlook on life and the level of perfection that he strives for. The overpowering nature of Leo is also an issue for Virgo who is generally smaller and more assertive. The couple is constantly at risk of personality clashes.

Leo is an unchangeable sign. Virgo is another sign that is mutable on the wheel of the zodiac. In this particular instance the relationships between them are typically marked by tension for both parties. In general, they must perform a significant work to be able to comprehend and help one another.

Their interactions in the field of work tend to be positive because every sign has unique capabilities and behaviors that may be beneficial in their interactions to the workplace. The Leo sign is known for its affinity to organization, while the Virgo sign is more inclined to analysis and organizational. When they're serious about it, they'll be able to accomplish numerous great things when they are together.

On a sentimental level, they are a bit tangled however, not difficult. The worst aspects of their relationship are the tendency to be the leader when it comes to Leo and the tendency to criticize when it comes to Virgo. But the most beneficial characteristic is usually complete sexual compatibility (not good, right?).

In the end, they are extremely intelligent and curious individuals. This is why it is not unusual for them to come across diverse points of convergence particularly intellectual ones which can help them get closer to the shores of their own.

Virgo with Virgo A relationship that is characterized by the possibility of conflicts of interest, as well as continuous criticism

Because of the nature that you are born with, you are inclined to look for the perfect details in all you do. And since your partner too is with that energy there are plenty of personality clashes since everyone wants to be accurate and right and to not succumb to criticism from one. It is possible to work but lots of perseverance is needed from both the sides.

Virgo is one of the signs that can be mutable in the zodiac. As such two people born under the same sign tend to be able to get along well since they share a variety of traits. The general consensus is that their compatibility is very high as they share a variety of personal traits both for good and worse.

They can be found well in the workplace since they share the same or similar goals and methods of interacting. Additionally one of the main characteristics that characterize Virgo is their pursuit of perfection. Often in a hurry, they review for hours and hours their work to ensure that they aren't making mistakes. This is precisely why they are able to achieve their goals (so that their commitment to work sooner or later typically will pay off).

In the field of affection, they are able to get along quite well because they share similar habits of mind and tastes in and acting. The issue with their relationship lies in their excessive reserve and does not give much room for surprises Their relationship runs the risk of becoming too boring. In the end the final word, in the event that Virgo does not like surprise, what else could she offer? They'll be delighted to be treated in this way.

Virgo with Libra A complicated relationship

Libra can be a highly social sign with loving groups and all sorts of activities in the outside world, however Virgo generally is reserved, methodical as well as less expressive this sense. The contradictions are apparent and will soon be apparent at the most inconvenient time.

Virgo is one of the mutable signs, and Libra is among the cardinals in the zodiac. In general their relationships are likely to enrich often whether they are conscious or not they realize that they've got a lot to share and learn from one another.

Collaboration is usually a regular feature when it is about the two signs working together. It is often Libra's turn to become the person who is pulling the cart however Libra will not take long to respond and begin working to the fullest extent. The main attraction of their partnership is often the difference that each symbolizes for the other and, as a result, they are able to complement one another completely, or even.

If they get married the relationship is generally sexy, among other reasons because they are two people who love perfection above all else, which is why they are always trying to improve their relationship.

At times your partner, just like all of us, could have the chance to fall into the feared routine, however Libra will ensure that this doesn't happen through provoking Virgo. They'll simply have having a diverse and full-bodied relationship, and each day. more perfect.

Virgo with Scorpio is a passionate love affair that is difficult

It could appear that because of the land-water connection it would be a perfect combination, but it's not. Although compatibility is not unattainable particularly if ascendants have a connection and have a common ancestor, the clash of personalities are intense. When it comes to love, it can be very intense however, other than the fact that Scorpio's egocentric nature and jealousy the dominance of his are in conflict with Virgo's analytical and critical character, resulting in difficult situations.

It is a sign that Virgo can be mutable within the zodiacal wheel. Scorpio is among the fixed signs within the wheel. In the majority of situations, their relationships create the perfect catalyst for each person needs to develop in all aspects of their lives. They are extremely effective in the professional world In addition, whether either consciously or not they realize that they can accomplish many things when they collaborate without affecting the work of the other.

Furthermore, loyalty influences their relationship. There is no limit to what can happen within their relationships, however they'll not lie sincerity is one of the greatest allies they can have, and even more so. Because of all of the mentioned above, your goals won't be far off in the future.

On a sentimental level the relationship between them is like the one in the previous case as well as higher. Virgo Scorpio and Scorpio represent the most comprehensive pair that can be found between two individuals to counteract the worst of each and increase the strengths of each.

Virgo gradually increases self-confidence and confidence with Scorpio near, who is then able to gain confidence in himself as well as in other people with Virgo at his side. In essence, they are the same for.

Virgo with Sagittarius and Sagittarius, a connection that is based on disagreements

Two temperaments with very distinct personalities. Sagittarius is lively free, unassuming, and loves to express themselves. Virgo prefers to be more reserved quiet, analytical and critical. Discussions are plentiful. Sagittarius would like to go to a bar, Virgo is content to be at home. Virgo is looking forward to going out one way and Sagittarius to the other. Getting them to agree is a challenge.

Virgo along with Sagittarius are two of the signs which are part of the mutable signs of the zodiac. But, contrary to what you might think the relationship between them is not generally good as the differences between them are vast. However it is imperative to consider their relatives to determine whether they'll be able to get along better or worse.

In the workplace relationships, they are likely to be unique, as their areas of work and interests tend to be distinct. Additionally the result could cause fatal consequences. Virgo is known for its disciplined work ethic. Sagittarius typically does not have. Bullfighters are the exception. In the same way, the zeal for perfection characteristic of Virgo is shattered by the erratic nature of Sagittarius and is overwhelmed by the perfectionists of his partner.

When they are a couple, they typically have issues, because their views of life do not match. Virgo has such a serene person that Sagittarius simply being at his close by can cause him to get agitated.

For his part this sign may feel threatened by Virgo close by And in the case of Sagittarius their freedoms are sacred. However Sagittarius is a sign that usually has an interesting and fluid communication, which is a crucial first step.

Virgo with Capricorn and Capricorn, a strong relationship

The two signs of the earth element demonstrate many similarities and compatibility. Industrious, serious, disciplined and responsible, they are able to recognize perfectly with everything, and there is a clear connection between them. Romantic relationships are lengthy and quiet.

Virgo is one of the Zodiac signs that are mutable and Capricorn is among the cardinal signs. In general their compatibility is extremely high since they share a number of positive aspects that are in common. At work their relationships are typically an ongoing exercise of cooperation.

The one and the other one show the respect they have towards the efforts of their respective Additionally they have an extraordinary sense of responsibility. They also have the same economic standards which means they don't be in conflict over this issue. Because of this, Virgo and Capricorn will succeed in what they have set out to accomplish with respect to their common interests.

If they become two couples, they have the chance to get to be friends, as they are aware of the individuality of each other perfectly. Virgo and Capricorn might not be the type of kindly words and constant kisses, but they'll demonstrate love for each other in various ways.

There is no room for lies in their marriage, and that's why they are so trusting and, without doubt their relationship, no matter it is, demonstrates a remarkable sincerity. In the end, Virgo and Capricorn will have high hopes for the future.

Virgo with Aquarius, a complex relationship

There are stark personality conflicts. Virgo is earth and Aquarius is air, and to top it off the perception of each is completely different. If something seems right, normal and suitable to you, your partner might find absurd and perhaps even absurd. In the same way it happens to you in the case of Aquarian issues. An uneasy relationship.

Virgo is one of the mutable signs on the zodiac wheel. The zodiac sign Aquarius is among those fixed significations. The relationships they have, the majority of instances, aren't bad as they enjoy excellent communication, despite the differences they exhibit.

Their connections are advantageous when it comes to work as they each have distinct abilities that could be extremely complementary. Aquarius is blessed with ability to come up with innovative ideas, while Virgo is a master of planning and organizing, that is the realization in a particular project and of the creating Aquarius. They also share with a remarkable level of ability to think, which is why they respect and admire each one another.

In terms of their relationships with each other The situation isn't clear, since at first, they aren't usually like they are able to be a couple in any way, because of their different personality.

However, Virgo and Aquarius do share a peculiar personality which makes them continuously experiment across different fields. Aquarius most of all, who enjoys adventure and by dragging Virgo along. And what is more thrilling than love?

Virgo with Pisces A relationship between opposite signs, with attraction

Pisces can be your sign opposite, and the relationship you have with it is a reflection of what the opposite poles attracting. It is possible to find a perfect partner in Pisces because they are able to accept criticism, and, in the end, they will be able to articulate their thoughts to your partner, leaving you speechless and amazed by the clarity of an insight derived from your inner knowledge of your character.

Virgo and Pisces are both a part of the same zodiacal traits that is their mutable nature. Yet they aren't always well balanced, as they're in opposite positions based on their individual personalities. Virgo is the most rational of things. Pisces is contrary utilizes intuition as a key engine. They are the representation of the difference between reason and intuition.

They have plenty at work If they have the passion to it. Two people have distinct characteristics. Unfortunately they don't always find themselves attracted when it comes to joining a group to fulfill a particular goal. Additionally, the different areas they traverse aren't connected to one another, which makes it difficult for them to get to know each other.

The relationships they have on a personal scale are not very happy, either, because the stability that is typical of this sign Virgo disappears when there is an unstable person like Pisces close by, which for Virgo is unsettling, maybe overly.

But, often they are enticed by an intense sexual desire that can unite them in love at times, but in the end, they all walk silently on other routes.

The 12 signs that have Virgo Ascendant

Aries Ascendant Virgo

The Aries male and Virgo rising This can make you extremely efficient when it comes to business. You're an energetic well-organized man. You are a competent manager who doesn't hesitate to put in the effort. While you're determined to achieve the desired results, but you shouldn't be shocked when you find yourself having to be better than you did. In your relationship it is important not to focus your attention on irrelevant details.

www.ingramcontent.com/pod-product-compliance
Lightning Source LLC
Chambersburg PA
CBHW050411120526
44590CB00015B/1920